# Messy In The Kitchen

## MY GUIDE TO EATING DELICIOUSLY, HOSTING FABULOUSLY AND SIPPING COPIOUSLY

## RENÉE PAQUETTE

PERMUTED
PRESS

A PERMUTED PRESS BOOK

ISBN: 978-1-68261-938-4

ISBN (eBook): 978-1-64293-930-9

*Messy in the Kitchen:*
*My Guide to Eating Deliciously, Hosting Fabulously and Sipping Copiously*

Photography by Gaby Duong (www.gabyduong.com)
Food Styling by Jackie Sobon
Cover Design by Manny Rosario (mannyrcreative.com)
Interior Design by Mark Karis
Edited by Jacob Hoye

This book contains information relating to the health benefits of certain ingredients. It should be used to supplement rather than replace the advice of your doctor or another trained health professional. All efforts have been made to ensure the accuracy of the information in this book as of the date of publication.

Renée Paquette is represented by MacGregor & Luedeke.

**PERMUTED**
**PRESS**

Permuted Press, LLC
New York • Nashville
permutedpress.com

*Published in the United States of America*
*Printed in Canada*
10 9 8 7 6 5 4 3 2 1

*To Jon and our sweet little baby. May our stomachs always be full, our glasses (or bottles) always be topped, and traditions a plenty. I love you guys. And the dogs, too. I love them. The future's looking good!*

# Contents

# Introduction

Holy crap, I can't believe this is happening and it's here! I manifested this so hard. I've wanted to make this cookbook for years! I actually had about half of it written before I ever got a book deal. I was just hoping and praying that if I put it out into the universe enough, someone else would also think this was a good idea. So here we are. You're now holding my book in your hands! What the hell?!

I've loved cooking for a very long time and was food obsessed long before that. I come from a family of capable home chefs and adventurous eaters.

There's literally nothing I won't at least try. You have no idea my level of excitement when I see a new chip flavor on display at the grocery store. That's my happy place. I also deeply appreciate experimenting with food, testing out what works in the kitchen, what excites my taste buds, and making adjustments on the fly. Unlike baking, which is actual science, I prefer the whimsical nature of not having to take this all so seriously. YOU CAN COOK! It just takes trial and error and taking it easy on yourself. Hey, you can always fall back on ordering a

1

pizza if your endeavor turns into an epic fail! Believe me, I've been there. When I first started doing this book, I felt that I knew my way around the kitchen pretty well, but now, having spent so much time testing recipes and re-making dishes, I've achieved a whole new level of confidence. Time spent in the kitchen is never a loss. At the very least, it means more experience under your belt!

We're all spending so much more time at home these days. And while Postmates and Uber Eats are genius ideas, and I love them a ton, nothing beats a home-cooked meal. And nothing tops the joy of cooking for other people. Is there anything more satisfying than having friends and family over, watching everyone take their first bite, and realizing you just nailed that meal? I don't think so. However, my husband is well over me staring at him while he tastes something I just made, my eyes full of hope and anticipation. It's a lot of pressure, I know. Just tell me it's good and I'll leave you alone!

One of my favorite things is having people over and feeding them an abundance of delicious food and copious cocktails. Happy, full, and tipsy! From hosting a BBQ, Friendsgiving, Christmas with a house full of family, or just having some drinks and snacks, I love when the house is packed with people. Loud and messy is my jam! But over years of figuring out how to orchestrate it, and getting better and better at it, I wanted to share with you some of my favorite recipes, tips, and tricks.

My biggest two tips are these: clean as you go and keep everyone's glass full.

Throughout this book I'll cover some of my favorite pantry staples—items I need on hand, and a backup just in case, kitchen utensils I live by, and recipes from breakfast to snacks to dinner, and some cocktails to round it all out.

If you follow me on Instagram or know me IRL, you know I'm a music junkie. Nothing gets my chakras aligned and my Zen just right like slow cooking a meal, sipping a glass of wine, and spinning some of my favorite artists. That's my church. So I've added a few playlists for your earhole's pleasure. I've reached out to some of my favorite people and they've helped me curate these playlists that I hope you thoroughly enjoy. So get ready to roll up your sleeves, pop a cork, and feed some mouths.

Thanks for taking the time to read my book. You have no idea how happy it makes me. For real.

# Kitchen Staples

Being on the road as frequently as I am, let me tell you, no matter where you've been in the world or how incredible a trip it might have been, there is nothing like returning to your own home, your own bed, your own shower, and most importantly, your own kitchen. I get so excited staring into the abyss that is my completely unorganized spice cupboards and jacked-up pantry and breathe a sigh of sweet relief that I can now cook my own meal, on my own time, in my own space. HEAVEN. Over the years I've obsessively added to my collection of spices and oils, splurging on some saffron-infused so-and-so or a beautiful CBD olive oil to top my dishes. But there are some items that I ALWAYS have on hand, and occasionally a backup juuuust in case. Here are some spices and tools that are guaranteed to give your meals a swift kick in the ass, or make you feel like the Ina Garten of your own household.

## SPICES AND SEASONINGS

Sea salt

Whole peppercorns, with a peppercorn grinder, of course (Trust me, it makes a huge difference over the pre-ground pepper.)

Red pepper chili flakes

A nice olive oil (Expensive isn't always the way, but you want one that tastes good on its own—no bitterness, no weird mouth residue, with a nice, clean finish.)

Maldon sea salt flakes. (I'm always amazed by the crunch and flavor these chunks add when sprinkled on top of a meal—a finishing salt if you will. Ohh la la! Most grocery stores sell it, but you can order it BY THE BUCKET online.)

Cayenne

Paprika (I love me a smoked paprika.)

Garlic powder

Onion powder

## UMAMINESS

Soy sauce

Fish sauce

Sriracha

Tomato paste

Aged parmesan wedge

## THE FRESH STUFF

Herbs (I would love to say I have a really adorable herb garden growing on my windowsill, but I have the complete opposite of a green thumb. Nothing lives in my house. So, fake plants it is. Actually, I should make a decoy fake herb garden. Anyway, green thumb or not, adding fresh herbs to your meals really takes it up to another level and I almost always have these on hand.)

Cilantro

Basil

Oregano

Dill

Rosemary

Lemons (Prepackaged lemon and lime juice can suck it.)

Garlic

Ginger

Green onions

Butter (Salted and unsalted.)

Milk or cream

Eggs

## DRIED AND CANNED GOODS

: Dry pasta

: Rice

: Quinoa

: Crushed tomatoes

## TOOLS

**Cast-iron skillet.** I use mine All. The. Time. I know they're not cheap, but they're a great investment. If you take care of it properly, you'll have it forever. Learn how to treat it, re-season it, wash it…or don't wash it. It distributes heat so much better than a standard pan, and there's simply nothing better for getting an insane crispness to your meats. You can even pop it in the oven to finish meals. Do yourself a favor and add one to your life! I personally love Lodge. This is not sponsored by Lodge, but I'm open to the conversation! (Hi, Lodge! I love you!)

**A great knife.** Same as a cast-iron skillet, it's an investment, and you have to take care of it, but it makes chopping stuff up so much more exciting! Remember to keep your fingers and extremities safe! A great, sharp knife is a game changer. Ever try chopping onions with a dull, crappy knife, and you're already crying because onions are wild like that, and it's taking even longer because the knife blows? Let's make that a thing of the past. The onions will still get ya, but it'll be way quicker. (Apparently if you freeze an onion you won't tear up, but I never remember this until the moment I need to chop an onion.) For a great

sharp, sturdy knife, my go-to brand is Grohmann Knives in Pictou, NS. My grandparents lived out in Nova Scotia and this great knife shop was down the street from them, and for Christmas or my birthday my mom usually hooks me up with a fancy new knife. Yes, these are the things you look forward to as an adult! If you don't have beloved family members in Nova Scotia, you can find these knives online.

**Cutting boards.** You'll need a nice big wooden one with a groove around the edge, to catch juices from meats hanging out to rest, and a simple plastic one.

I love a good set of **wooden spoons**, but they're not make or break.

I used my **measuring spoons** religiously while making this book, but that was literally just so I sounded like I knew what I was talking about. I mostly eyeball stuff and go by taste, so feel free to do the same and make these dishes your own. It's meant to be fun and relaxing, so trust your instincts!

# Breakfast

The meal that starts the day and sets the tone. Is there any smell better than bacon crisping up in a hot pan? Absolutely not. Is there a better sight than a runny yolk? The things I would do for a perfectly cooked runny egg, slathered up on a piece of buttered toast or a fluffy pastry. Drool City, USA. I've got you covered. Whether you and your pals tore it up the night before and need some carbs and a mimosa or you're about to tackle the millions of things piled up on your to-do list…you can't do that on an empty stomach. Not on my watch!

"FAST FOOD I THINK IS LIKE A CONSPIRACY, Y'KNOW? I THINK THAT'S HOW THEY JUST KEEP US DUMB. YOU CAN'T EVEN THINK AFTER A WHILE, YOU EVER NOTICE THAT SH**? LIKE YOU EVER HAD YOUR WHOLE DAY PLANNED OUT, YOU EAT ONE EGG MCMUFFIN AND YOU'RE JUST ON THE COUCH, 'EH, Y'KNOW WHAT, F*** MY DREAMS.'"

—BILL BURR

# OVERNIGHT BREAKFAST CASSEROLE

*Serves 6–8*

Here's why I love an overnight casserole: all the work is done the night before, maybe when you're like three glasses of wine in, so things are hazy at best. This is a real winner when you have a house full of guests looking at you to whip them something up to eat in the morning. Even though the red wine has reared its ugly head and you're tired and wine puffy, you still get to feel like Betty freaking Crocker when you remember that drunk gift you prepared for yourself, this life-saver. Just pop it in the oven and pour yourself a very large coffee.

16 oz. loaf of crusty bread (about 8 cups torn into cubes by hand)

10 slices thick-cut bacon, diced

1 shallot, thinly sliced

8 eggs

½ cup cream

¼ cup maple syrup

2 cups cheddar cheese

butter or cooking spray for the baking dish

maple syrup to serve

1. Slice the bacon into 1-inch chunks and crisp in a pan. Drain most of the bacon grease but leave a small amount to fry the thinly sliced shallots until brown and crispy.

2. Grease a 9x12 baking dish. Tear the bread into roughly 1-inch cubes with your hands. Add the bacon and shallots. Whip the eggs, cream, and maple syrup together, then soak the bread in it. Mash it down with your hands, get a little messy, and make sure all of the bread gets a good dose of this eggy goodness. Top with 2 cups of shredded cheddar. Cover and place in the fridge overnight.

3. When you're ready to feast, pop this guy in the oven at 350 degrees for about 40 minutes, when the cheese is bubbly and beginning to brown. Serve with maple syrup for a salty-sweet combo!

**SEMI PRO TIP:** *A little hair of the dog never hurt anyone. Get yourself a mimosa!*

# CINNAMON ROLLS

*Makes 12 rolls*

I felt strongly that it was my duty to perfect the cinnamon roll. When I first started writing this book, I really wasn't one for doughs or baking or waiting for a stupid yeast to rise. But I feel like I've spent enough time over the past year or so working with these finicky single-cell microorganisms that I am no longer intimidated by them. So, time to let the yeast rise, roll it out, rise it again, and bake it for the best payoff of all time: a tray of warm ooey gooey cinnamon rolls. You'll become everyone's favorite family member / friend / co-worker / Uber driver. Pssssst: the secret ingredient is adding a little cardamom. What a fun, cool, underutilized spice. Just a touch, and it gives these rolls a little *je ne sais quoi*.

| | | |
|---|---|---|
| 1 cup warm milk | 1½ cups brown sugar | ½ cup softened unsalted butter |
| ½ cup white sugar | 2 tbsp. ground cinnamon | 8oz. softened cream cheese |
| .25-oz. packet active dry yeast | 1 tsp. cardamom | 1 cup powdered sugar |
| 4 cups all-purpose flour | ½ cup softened salted butter | ¼ cup half and half |
| 2 room-temperature eggs | | ¼ tsp. salt |
| 1 tsp. vanilla extract | | |
| 5 tbsp. melted butter | | |

1. Begin by warming the milk on the stove or in a microwave for 30 seconds at a time. You don't want the milk to be hot. You want it warm to the touch before you add the yeast, or it won't activate properly. Before you add the yeast, dissolve the sugar in the milk. Then add the yeast and allow to sit for about 5 minutes until it becomes creamy and frothy.

2. In a smaller bowl, whisk together the eggs and the vanilla extract. The eggs need to be at room temperature. You can warm them in a bowl of warm water until ready to use if you forgot to take them out of the fridge in advance. I'm definitely guilty of that from time to time.

3.  In a large mixing bowl or stand mixer with the dough hook attachment, add the flour and melted butter. (Do not add the butter while hot because it'll mess with the yeast. Let it cool down a bit. Dough is weird and specific. Science.) Then add the egg/vanilla mixture, and the milk/yeast mixture. Stir to combine and knead into a ball. If it feels too wet, add a tablespoon of flour at a time until the consistency is right. You want it sticky but not wet. And it should bounce back some when you're kneading it. In a separate, greased bowl, add the dough, cover, and allow to rise until about doubled in size. Usually about an hour to an hour and a half.

4.  In a smaller bowl combine the brown sugar, cinnamon, and cardamom. Set aside.

5.  When the dough is ready and doubled in size, on a floured surface start to roll out the dough to a square shape, roughly 18x18 inches and about ¼ inch thick. With a rubber spatula or spoon, evenly spread the ½ cup (8 tbsp.) of soft butter. Don't use melted butter here, make sure it's at room temperature or else it all just leaks out. Sprinkle the brown sugar, cinnamon, cardamom mixture evenly over the buttered dough. Now it's time to roll! Fairly tightly, start to roll the dough into a log. Now cut the buns. Using a serrated knife, cut 12 evenly sliced rolls roughly 1½ inches thick. Place them cut side down in a greased 9x13 baking dish. Cover the dish with a damp cloth and allow to rise again for about 40 minutes.

6.  Set the oven to 400 degrees and bake for about 20 minutes. Once they are golden, take them out and allow to cool.

7.  For the icing, whip together the butter, cream cheese, icing sugar, and cream. Spread evenly over the cinnamon rolls. Mission accomplished, now time to attempt to not eat the entire tray in one sitting.

**SEMI PRO TIP**: Getting the temperatures right at the beginning of the process is the key to these babies turning out perfect. Bring the milk to a simmer so the sugar can dissolve in it thoroughly, but make sure you let it cool before you add the yeast, otherwise the yeast won't activate properly. Same with the eggs and melted butter. You want everything to be warm, not hot, not cold. It helps it all come together when you combine everything.

As a non-baker this was the recipe I tinkered with the most, and truly these changes make all the difference in the world for perfectly fluffy, soft cinnamon buns.

Using a serrated knife to slice the rolls is best. That way you won't squish them down when you're dividing them!

# SWEET POTATO HASH

*Serves 4*

What more is there really to say here? It's a delicious combo of *BAM!* (don't sue me, Emeril) sweet potatoes, a savory crunchy bite of bacon, and a runny yolk, all baked together in one dish. It makes for a solid breakfast, lunch, or dinner. Plus, it comes together super easy and leaves everyone full for hours! I respect a good, hearty, stick-to-your-ribs meal!

4 cups sweet potato, peeled and cubed (about 2 medium sweet potatoes)

1 cup yellow onion, diced

1 cup red pepper, diced

2 garlic cloves

6 slices thick-cut bacon, cubed

1 tsp. salt

½ tsp. pepper

1 tsp. paprika

½ tsp. garlic powder

5 large eggs

green onion, chopped for topping

1. In a large pan, ideally a cast-iron skillet, cook the bacon through until crispy, approximately 5–8 minutes. Remove from the pan and set aside, leaving the bacon grease in the pan.

2. Add the onions and garlic to the bacon grease, and cook until they are just starting to soften, about 3–5 minutes. Add the red pepper and cook for a few more minutes. Add the sweet potato, salt, pepper, garlic powder, and paprika. Toss to coat and place a lid over your pan. Stir occasionally until the potatoes begin to soften. Try not to move them too much, though, because you want the potatoes to crisp. About 15–20 minutes until cooked through. Remove from heat.

3. Crack 5 large eggs over the hash. Turn your oven on to broil. Place skillet in the oven on the middle rack to cook the eggs. About 3–5 minutes, depending on how runny you want your yolks to be. I like a runny yolk, so about 3 minutes will do it.

4. Top with some freshly chopped green onion or chives. Serve immediately.

# THE SCOTCH EGG

*Serves 6*

There's something very, very special about a hard-cooked egg enveloped in a greasy sausage hug. This definitely qualifies as a breakfast situation, but obviously eggs are good at all hours of the day. It infuriates me when I go to a restaurant and they've stopped serving breakfast at 10:00 a.m. I know you have the ingredients back there. It takes approximately 2 minutes to fry an egg and butter some toast. GIVE ME MY EGGS, YOU COWARDS! Anyway, I digress. I got this from my Nanny's recipe book. Instead of Monarch Chicken Crisp—I have no idea what that is—I swapped it out for some Shake 'n Bake, babaaaaayyyyyy. Seemed like something my Nanny would have approved of. Old School!

6 eggs

1 lb. ground sausage, or cut sausages from casings

1 packet Shake 'n Bake

1. Preheat the oven to 375 degrees

2. In a pot of boiling water, carefully add your eggs and boil for 10–12 minutes for hard yolks. You can't have no runny-yolk Scotch egg.

3. Meanwhile, knead your pork (lol) so you can smooth it around the egg.

4. Once your eggs are cooked, allow them to cool, or run under cold water, before removing the shells.

5. Divide the pork into 6 equal portions. In your hand, flatten the pork into a patty, about ¼ inch thick. Place the egg in the middle and wrap the sausage around to seal the edges together. Roll your sausage/egg combo in Shake 'n Bake to coat. Repeat with remaining eggs.

6. Place in the oven on a foil lined baking sheet for 25–30 minutes. They should be browned and crispy!

# CURRY EGGS IN HEAVEN

*Serves 4*

This cool guy makes for a killer breakfast, lunch, or dinner and comes together in about 30 minutes. The warmth of the curry, turmeric, and cumin makes my mouth water! I just love the smell of curry cooking in my house. I love me a good scented candle, but nothing really compares to the smell of a good home-cooked meal. FILL MY NOSTRILS UP! The curry combined with the coconut milk, partnered with poached eggs in this heavenly sauce, and sopped up with some crusty bread—leaves me in egg purgatory forever. This is the kind of meal that's best served in the skillet, with everyone digging in family style. Don't be shy. I'm a notorious double dipper. Zero shame.

| | |
|---|---|
| 2 tbsp. olive oil | 1½ tbsp. curry powder |
| ½ yellow onion, diced | ½ tbsp. turmeric powder |
| 1 garlic clove, minced | ½ tbsp. cumin powder |
| 2 inches fresh ginger, finely grated—about 1 tbsp. | ½ tsp. salt |
| | 6 large eggs |
| 1 can coconut milk (13.5 oz.) | ½ tsp. harissa to top |
| 1 can crushed tomatoes in their juices (13.5 oz.) | 1 bunch cilantro |
| | slices of crusty bread |

1. In a cast-iron skillet, heat the olive oil and add the onions over medium heat. Cook until they start to become translucent. Then add the garlic and ginger. Cook until fragrant—a minute or so.

2. Add the can of tomatoes and the coconut milk and bring to a simmer. Add the curry powder, turmeric powder, cumin, and salt. Allow to simmer on medium/low for about 20–25 minutes to reduce the sauce.

3. Once the sauce begins to thicken, create a little hole in the sauce with a wooden spoon and crack your egg. Continue this process with the rest of the eggs. Simmer the eggs for about 4 minutes, then put a lid over the skillet for a minute or two to set the tops of the eggs. Remove from heat. Top with a sprinkle of harissa and finish with some fresh cilantro.

4. For the crusty bread, set your oven to broil. Cut your loaf into 1-inch-thick slices, and coat each with a thin layer of olive oil. Pop in the oven on a baking sheet for 3–5 minutes on the middle rack until perfectly toasty.

5. SOAK UP THAT CURRY EGG COMBO ON THAT BREAD, Y'ALL.

SEMI PRO TIP: I recommend cooking this in a cast-iron skillet as the heat just distributes so much more evenly, which is ideal for poaching the eggs. And you can pop on the lid for a few minutes at the end to cook the eggs to perfect yolky tenderness, without any weird raw egg white.

# EGGS IN SNOW

*Depending on the number of mouths you have to feed—it's basically 2 eggs per slice of toast.*

I've got to give the credit for this recipe to my mom. Carole whips this thing up during the holidays, because a. it's freaking delicious, and b. it's the perfect quick breakfast to feed a crowd. All you have to do is line a baking sheet with as many slices of toast as you can cram on there, pile on the delicious fluffy egg white peaks, plop on the yolk, and jazz it up with whatever fun things you have on hand—ham, bacon, tomatoes, fancy cheese, green onion. You can go nuts, or just enjoy this simple delicacy as is. Toss it in the oven, and voila! Everyone has their own runny-egg toast situation to sop up the wine you consumed the night before.

eggs

toast

cheese

1. Set the oven to 375 degrees.

2. Toast the bread in a toaster. It's okay if it gets a bit cold. It's going back in the oven anyway. You just need the bread to be sturdy and crusty before piling on the eggs.

3. Separate your egg whites and yolks. I find it's easiest to separate the whites right into the bowl you're going to be whipping them up in and leave the individual yolks in their shell until you're ready to use them.

4. I whip up the egg whites in my stand mixer on high using the whisk attachment. It only takes a few minutes to reach optimal fluffy cloud-like peaks. I let the stand mixer do its thing while I prep the rest of the meal, grate the cheese and line the baking sheet with aluminum foil. If you don't have a stand mixer, you can use a hand mixer to fluff!

5. Once your egg whites are fluffy and airy, and your baking sheet is lined with the slices of toast, you're ready to make these little egg dreams become a reality. Pile the egg whites high on the toast, don't be shy! Dig out a little hole in the egg whites and drop your yolk into the center. You don't want it to slip off, so make sure the hole is deep enough to hold the yolk. Sprinkle with salt and pepper, then add a healthy dose of grated cheese on top.

6. If you want to add meat, or veggies, or whatever your little heart desires, go for it. I would suggest putting the additional toppings on the toast first and then building the egg cloud on top of that.

7. Pop these little babies in the oven for about 10–12 minutes until the egg white is crispy and the yolk is cooked to your desired doneness.

8. Enjoy!

SEMI PRO TIP: Highly recommend for a crowd! Minimal work and clean up, and lots of happy, full people.

# Snacks & Such

I am the type of person that basically doesn't stop eating. Snack Queen should be tattooed on my lower back. I like to tell myself that if I graze continually throughout the day then that should technically just keep my metabolism running like the Tesla that it is. Right? So, let us embark on a journey of snacks and treats and light meals.

"MY WEAKNESSES HAVE ALWAYS BEEN FOOD AND MEN—IN THAT ORDER."

—DOLLY PARTON

# BLOODY MARY DEVILED EGGS

*Makes 12*

I tried to combine my love of deviled eggs with my love of everyone's favorite morning cocktail. A spin on the classic with a little zip of Bloody Mary mix topped off with a dash of celery salt and a chunk of crispy salty bacon! I ALWAYS use Mr. And Mrs. T's Bloody Mary mix, both for this recipe and in any Bloody Mary I make. It's the brand that's used on most airlines, so I have fond memories of sipping on these babies miles up in the air trying not to outwardly sob to *Marley & Me* for the one hundredth time. Same goes for *My Girl*. Why do I like to drink and cry on a plane? I'm not a doctor, but it's gotta be something to do with the altitude. Some people join the mile-high club (is that a real thing? I'd have a panic attack trying to get it on in the tiny, always-soaked lavatory); I prefer the "let's drink and weep club!" Anyways, enjoy these eggs!

6 large eggs

¼ cup mayonnaise

2 tbsp. Bloody Mary mix

½ tsp. mustard

½ tsp. lemon juice

¼ tsp. pepper

2 slices of bacon

celery salt

1. Carefully lower your eggs into a pot of enough boiling water to completely cover the eggs. Boil for 12–14 minutes

2. Fry your bacon until crispy over medium-high heat. Remove from the pan and allow to cool, then break into 2-inch pieces with your hands. Reserve for the garnish!

3. Once your eggs are cooled, remove the shells and slice in half with a sharp knife. Place the egg whites on your serving plate, and in a separate bowl add the yolk and begin to mash with a fork. Add the mayo, mustard, pepper, lemon juice, and Bloody Mary mix. Mix until smooth. You don't need to add extra salt here because the celery salt adds a little kick for the garnish, but if you're not going to use celery salt, then salt and pepper to taste.

4. Carefully spoon the yolk mixture back into the egg whites, garnish with a sprinkle of celery salt and a nice chunk of that crispy bacon!

5. Refrigerate until ready to serve.

# CLAM CHOWDER POUTINE

*Serves 4–6*

Poutine is my country's dish, possibly the thing all Canadians can form an instant connection over. Well, poutine, Mike Myers, and strong beer. Poutine is what I would confidently refer to as a perfect dish. Traditionally, it's fries, cheese curds (it NEEDS to be curds!) and a brown beef gravy, but I wanted to give this tried, tested, and true classic a seafood spin, because I love all foods from the sea. You can give this East Coast chowder version a spin or go with the OG. I'm giving you both versions. Or you can just have clam chowder. Or you can just have fries. Whatever floats your poutine gravy boat. It's like a choose-your-own-adventure book for fries.

## FOR THE CHOWDAH

Keep in mind this recipe is made for the poutine, so I left out the baby potatoes, because that's too many potatoes, even for me! If you're just making the chowder, I'd add the potatoes—about 2 cups of halved baby potatoes. Add them in after all the liquid is simmering. Cook until soft, about 10–12 minutes.

8 slices of bacon, cut into 1-inch pieces (You'll only need 6 if you're just making the chowder, but cook extra and use it as a topping. More bacon has literally never been a bad thing throughout the history of mankind.)

1 cup onions, diced

2 cloves of garlic, minced

1 tbsp. unsalted butter

⅓ cup flour

½ cup dry white wine

1 cup milk

2 cups chicken stock

1 cup half and half

2 tsp. fresh thyme (1 tsp. if you're using dried thyme)

2 bay leaves

3 cans chopped clams, plus their juice (6.5 oz. cans)

2 green onion stalks, diced

¼ cup all-purpose flour

⅓ cup water

1. In a large pot, cook the bacon until crispy, remove about ⅓ of the bacon so you can top either your poutine or the chowder with it.

2. With the remaining bacon and its fat drippings, start to cook the onions and garlic until soft. About 3–5 minutes. Add the thyme and bay leaves and cook until aromatic. Add the butter, and, once it's melted, start to slowly add the flour. It will get really thick, but that's okay. You're about to add the wine! Once you're ready to add the wine, continue to stir the mixture until you can smell the alcohol cooking out of the wine. It only takes a few minutes. Then add the milk, chicken stock, and half and half. Bring it back to a simmer. Add the clams and their clammy juices. Allow to simmer for about 10 minutes. To thicken the soup, mix together ¼ cup of flour and ⅓ cup of water to make a slurry, and slowly mix it into the soup. It will thicken almost immediately. Discard the bay leaves before serving.

3. Top with crispy bacon and green onion.

## FRIES(!!)

8 large russet potatoes, cut into ½-inch-thick sticks

2 quarts canola oil

Salt

Deep fry thermometer

1. Wash the potatoes. If you're not into the skin, peel it off. I always prefer to leave the skins on. Cut them into fry shapes!

2. Place your potatoes in a large bowl and rinse with cold water. After they've been rinsed, fill the bowl up with cold water and let the potatoes hang in there for at least an hour. We want to get all of the extra starch out of the potatoes so they're nice and crispy when we fry them.

3. Drain the potatoes and dry off with a paper towel. Get them as dry as you can.

4. In a deep fryer or a Dutch oven, add the canola oil and bring it to 320 degrees. This is where the thermometer is necessary—because you'll fry the potatoes twice. Once to start the frying at a lower temperature and then the second time, at a higher temperature, to crisp them up!

5. In batches, carefully add the potatoes. Don't crowd the pot. Allow them to cook for about 5 minutes, until they begin to turn golden. Remove them from the oil and allow to drain on a paper towel lined baking sheet.

6. Bring the heat back up between batches. The temperature naturally lowers when you add the potatoes to the oil. Once all of the potatoes have been in their first oil bath, bring the oil up to 400 degrees. Add the potatoes in batches again, and cook for about 5 minutes again, until golden brown and crispy!

7. Sprinkle with salt and whatever toppings and flavors you're into.

## FRY TOPPINGS

- sea salt and rosemary
- truffle oil
- garlic and parmesan
- old Bay

To assemble the poutine, place your hot fries on a plate or in a bowl, add a handful of cheese curds, and top with the clam chowder. You want everything hot, so the cheese curds melt. Finish with crispy bacon and green onions on top.

## FOR THE POUTINE

- 16 oz. white cheese curds
- hot fries
- clam chowder

# REGULAR-ASS POUTINE

Just in case you freaked out at the clam chowder poutine, I'm gonna go ahead and leave this right here so you can make a traditional poutine! Piping hot fries, cheese curds, and this heavenly brown gravy. This gravy is also a great backup if you don't get enough beef dripping from a roast, or want to top some mashed potatoes, or simply want some gravy in your life. I am not here to judge; I am here to provide you the goods. This is super simple and ready in minutes!

| | |
|---|---|
| 2 cups beef stock. Not broth. I repeat, not broth. | ½ tsp. pepper |
| | 1 tsp. beef bouillon |
| 2 tbsp. butter | ¼ cup water |
| ½ tsp. onion powder | 2 tbsp. flour |
| ¼ tsp. salt | |

1. Bring the beef stock to a simmer and add the butter, onion powder, salt, and bouillon.

2. In a bowl, whisk together the water and flour to create a slurry. Slowly add it to the beef stock. It will begin to thicken right away. Allow to simmer on low for about 5 minutes. Salt and pepper to taste.

SPICY BLACKBERRY
JALAPENO PRESERVES

FRESH HONEYCOMB
I'M WEIRDLY OBSESSED
WITH THIS WAXY TEXTURE

HARD SALAMI

CAPICOLA

BRIE CHEESE
A HUGE CROWD PLEASER
SERVE SOFT AT ROOM TEMPERATURE

STINKY CHEESE
A VEINY GORGONZOLA

FRESH HERBS TO
DRESS UP THE PLATE

ROLLED PROSCUITTO

GRAPES, STRAWBERRIES,
BLUEBERRIES, RASPBERRIES,
DRIED APRICOTS ADD FRESHNESS

CANNED ROASTED CODFISH
HARD CHEESE MANCHEGO

BALSAMIC
BELLAVITANO CHEESE

MIXED SPICY
NUTS FOR CRUNCH

ITALIAN DRY
SALAMI

SMOKED
CHEDDAR

BARSIN CHEESE
(BURY ME WITH A
SLAB OF THIS CHEESE)

HI BENNY!

PRETTY CANNED FISH
ADD A POP OF ART TO YOUR TRAY
MUNDO FANTASTICO DA
SAROLINHA PORTUGUESA

# THE ART OF THE CHARCUTERIE

I'm going on the record right now to profess my love of Lunchables, from elementary school lunches to driving from town to town between shows. Every gas station sells them. They've always been there for me, through the good times and the bad. I love you, Lunchables, my beginner's guide to charcuterie.

Let me tell you all of the ways in which I am head over heels in love with a charcuterie board. 1. It's casual AF so, once it's assembled, everyone can just gather round and help themselves. Perfect when you're hosting friends and family. 2. It's a pile of meats, cheese, crackers, and other sweet little delicacies, covering pretty much all of the food groups! 3. You can sneakily consume 15,000 calories of cheese and no one will even notice because they're busy concocting their own menagerie of goods.

When you're planning on doing a charcuterie, think about what delicious cured meats everyone will like, pick a variety of cheeses, and then add the fun little accoutrements that can take your cracker/ meat/cheese situation up a level. I love piling on some pickled vegetables and fruit, like apricots, berries, or grapes, to add some sweetness to your palate. A bit of freshness goes a long way. Add sauces as well, maybe a grainy mustard, a berry compote, or spicy honey. I love adding a chunk of honeycomb. It looks pretty and adds a cool texture.

## MEATS

I like an array of salty meats, cured meats, and fresh shaved deli meats. ALWAYS add a pâté of some sort. I could live off liverwurst. It's on every tray I've ever made. Anyone who is freaked out by it obviously has never tried it!

Here are some meats to consider: prosciutto, hard salami, mortadella, soppressata, and capicola. All of these are usually bought pre-sliced and easy to splay out on your board. Rolling the thinly sliced pieces into little tubes or arranging in loosely folded pieces makes for easy picking,

**Pâté:** I always have a log of Farmer John liverwurst on deck, but Sells chicken liver pâté or smoked salmon or crab pâté is a great unexpected addition.

**Canned Fish:** Oh baby! I brought SO much canned fish back from Portugal when I went. The tins can be so pretty and really add a visual pop to your board. The name of the company is Comur and you can order it online. IT'S DECADENT! Some other great companies to check out are Patagonia Provisions, Taylor Shellfish Farms, La Gondola, and Da Morgada. I want to frame these cans. They're so, so pretty!

## CHEESES

We want mild, soft, hard, stinky, creamy…and I love adding in a wild card of something infused or just straight-up experimental. There are always tons of options at the grocery store to try out! But think texture, too. You want some cheeses that are spreadable, some on the firm side, and something that can be sliced. You don't need to check off each category, but a variety in texture and taste is great!

**Mild:** Brie, Camembert, Asiago, Havarti, goat cheese

**Soft:** Brie, goat cheese, Gournay cheese. You're going to want to be sure these are served at room temperature for optimal spreadability.

**Stinky:** blue cheese, Gorgonzola, Roquefort. Just check the ages and the intensity of the blue veins running through the cheese. That's usually a good indicator of what level of cheese stink you're dealing with.

**Hard:** Parmigiano Reggiano, Manchego, Pecorino Romano

**Infused:** truffle Gouda, cheddar cheese with porter beer, whole grain mustard cheese, balsamic, Cajun; there's just so many to choose from. Get adventurous!

## EXTRAS

**Fruit:** grapes, dried apricots, blueberries, apple slices, pear slices—any fresh seasonal fruit will do.

**Sauces:** grainy mustard, spicy or regular honey, a fruit compote or jam, tapenade, hummus, tzatziki, chutney

**Extras:** pickles, pickled veggies, olives, roasted garlic cloves, sun-dried tomatoes

**Nuts:** roasted cashews, almonds, spicy candied pecans

## CRACKERS/BREAD

I usually put out an assortment of crackers. Soda crackers, herb-infused crackers, sliced baguette, hell, I love me a Triscuit. I usually err on the side of a mild cracker to let the cheese and meats take center stage. We don't need to go crazy with too many flavors.

## ARRANGEMENT

I imagine myself creating a piece of art with meat and cheese, a paint-by-color of food, if you will! I love finding ways to display everything for maximum visual impact. Some of it can be pre-cut and sliced, for ease of accessibility. Or you can jam a cute little cheese knife right into the cheese for people to help themselves. Add little jars or ramekins for the sauces, fruits, nuts, and pickles. You can even make or purchase little name cards to label the cheeses. Once, during Christmas, I turned my entire dining table into a gigantic charcuterie. It's meant to be informal and loosey-goosey, so have fun and get creative!

SEMI PRO TIP: Keep in mind it's usually about 3-4 oz. per person, for when you're mapping out your charcuterie board.

# TURKEY PESTO TWISTS

*Serves 5*

Welcome to a dreamy combo that's easy as all hell to put together, yet looks fancy-ish and packs a punch! Pesto is a crowd pleaser. It's the most difficult part of this whole operation, but it is ridiculously easy to make. So, roll up your sleeves and get ready for some savory puffy snacks! You can also keep the leftover pesto in the fridge for up to 3 weeks. Toss it in pasta, add it to sandwiches, or make a caprese salad. Use that pesto up!

## FOR THE PESTO

- ½ cup pine nuts
- 1 garlic clove
- 1 cup olive oil
- 4 cups fresh basil leaves
- 1 cup parmesan (fresh is the best, but use what ya got!)
- ¼ tsp. salt
- ¼ tsp. pepper

## FOR THE TWISTS

- 1 sheet of puff pastry
- 4 pieces sliced turkey
- 1 tbsp. grated parmesan
- 1 egg
- 1 tbsp. water

1. Preheat the oven to 400 degrees.

2. Make your pesto! In a food processor or blender combine the pine nuts, garlic, olive oil, and basil leaves. Pulse together until smooth. Salt and pepper to taste.

3. Bring the puff pastry to just about room temperature. You want to keep it cold but thawed enough that you can work with it and it won't crack.

4. Evenly spread 3–4 tablespoons of pesto all over the puff pastry. Cover with an even layer of the turkey slices. If necessary, pop your puff pastry/pesto/turkey situation in the fridge or freezer for 5–10 minutes before you cut and twist them. It makes the puff pastry easier to work with.

5. Line a baking sheet with parchment paper.

6. With a sharp knife or, even better, a sharp pizza cutter (cutting things with a pizza slicer is very, very satisfying) evenly slice the puff pastry into 5 pieces, about 2 inches wide. Carefully twist the ends in opposite directions and place on the baking sheet.

7. In a small bowl, mix your egg with the tablespoon of water to make the egg wash. Brush the tops of the puff pastry with the egg wash and sprinkle with fresh parmesan.

8. Pop these bad boys in the oven for 15–20 minutes until golden brown.

TURKEY PESTO TWISTS

FRIED LOBSTER TAILS

JAMMY TOMATOES
ON TOAST

# FRIED LOBSTER TAILS ON A STICK

*Serves 2–4*

HOLD ONTO YOUR BUTTS. I've taken lobster tails, already a luxury too good for this earth, shoved them onto a stick, and then fried them in a CHAMPAGNE batter. Let's all embrace and get gout together. Let's make gout hot again, take the pirate's disease but make it fashion, and then fry it. It's like a fancy corndog…or…something? Anyways, let's talk about this batter. I was up to my nipples in beer batter while working on the perfect concoction, and I thought, *Ya know what we need? MORE bubbles.* I insist on always having a bottle of champagne in the fridge. You never know who might show up. The key here is using a dry champagne. Don't break the bank obvs, but dry is the way. (That's not what she said! Hahahkjsdfkjshfjahfla,) And keep the batter cold! Keep it in the fridge until you're ready to go. Here we go!

| | |
|---|---|
| ½ cup flour | 4 lobster tails |
| 1 tsp. salt | 1 lemon |

| | |
|---|---|
| 1 cup flour | 1 quart vegetable or canola oil |
| 1 tsp. salt | candy/oil thermometer |
| 1 egg, beaten | deep pan for frying—ideally cast iron or |
| 12 oz. dry champagne | Dutch oven so the oil heats evenly |
| 1 tbsp. fresh tarragon, finely chopped (optional) | bamboo skewers |

1. Let's heat that oil. In your pan, you need about 3 inches of oil. Canola or vegetable is best as they have the higher smoke point for frying. I like to use a high-temperature thermometer to accurately tell the temperature. Bring the oil to 375 degrees. If you don't have a high-temperature thermometer, you can place a drop of the batter in the oil to hear if it sizzles right away.

2. Time to set up our dredging stations! In one bowl, combine the ½ cup of flour and 1 tsp. of salt. In another bowl mix together the 1 cup of flour, salt, eggs, champagne, and tarragon, if you're using it.

3. Right about now is a perfect time to pour yourself some champagne while you're at it. You deserve it. Clap, clap, clap, clap.

4. Break those tails outta their shells. Run your knife along the back of the shell and crack the knife down to get to that sweet, sweet lobster meat.

5. Insert the bamboo skewers into the lobster tails.

6. Working one at a time, dredge the lobster tails in the flour/salt mix, shake off excess, and move on to the champagne batter. You want the lobster tails fully and evenly coated.

7. CAREFULLY place these suckers in the heated oil. Frying at home can be scary as all hell, but slow and steady and you've got this, giiiiiiirrrrrlllllll. Drop the lobster tails in slowly so not to splash the oil.

8. Fry the tails 4–5 minutes, turning halfway through.

9. Remove from the oil with tongs and allow to cool on a wire rack. This will keep the batter crispy.

10. Squeeze some fresh lemon juice over the lobster tails and sprinkle with flakey salt.

**SEMI PRO TIP**: Food on a stick is scientifically proven to taste better. I'm here for the facts. I've played a journalist on TV for years. Trust me.

# JAMMY TOMATOES—ON TOASTS

These babies change the tomato game. I love tomatoes so much and will never understand people that claim they don't like them. It makes me question their opinion on everything else henceforth. Weirdos. Anyway, this recipe is so simple that once you commit the time to slow roasting these little cuties you can give them the call up to a bunch of different meals. Add them to eggs, toss them in pasta, salads, make a face mask out of them…whatever floats your boat. (Don't actually make a face mask.) But smearing them on these little crostinis with some goat cheese and fresh basil is very pleasing to my tastehole.

| | |
|---|---|
| 1 pint of cherry or grape tomatoes | baguette |
| 4 tbsp. olive oil | 4 oz. goat cheese |
| 2 garlic cloves, minced | basil |
| ½ tsp. salt | |
| ¼ tsp. pepper | |

1. Preheat oven to 250 degrees. Slow 'n' low, y'all.

2. On a foil-lined baking sheet, combine the tomatoes, olive oil, garlic, salt, and pepper. Toss to coat the tomatoes well.

3. Put them in the oven for 2½–3 hours. After the first hour, give them a quick stir every 30 minutes.

4. The tomatoes will start to burst and the sugar in them will start to caramelize. Omg, you're so close to the big payoff. KEEP GOING! Take them out of the oven and switch the oven to broil.

5. Slice your baguette into 1-inch-thick pieces. Give a little drizzle of olive oil and toast the slices in the oven. Keep an eye on these guys, only about 1 minute per side.

6. Add a nice layer of goat cheese to the toast, about 1 tbsp. Add the tomatoes and top with some fresh torn basil.

# ROSEMARY SNACK MIX

Trader Joe's makes this incredible rosemary mixed-nut situation during the holidays and it's always a huge hit in the Paquette/Good/Moxley household. Problem is, it's seasonal, and we get hit with these cravings all year long. So here we are, just two young lovers looking for a rosemary snack mix. I added in some extras because standard bar snack mix is also a staple in this home. Two birds, one snack mix.

2 cups mixed, unsalted, blanched nuts. Literally whatever nuts you want. Or you can stick with one type of nut. I did a mixture of peanuts, pecans, cashews, almonds, and hazelnuts.

1 cup pretzels

1 cup Chex cereal

½ cup unsalted butter

4 tbsp. finely minced fresh rosemary

1 tsp. garlic powder

1. Preheat your oven to 300 degrees, and line a baking sheet with parchment paper

2. Melt half a cup of butter and add the rosemary and garlic powder. Mix well.

3. In a large mixing bowl, add the nuts, pretzels, and Chex, then toss with the butter mixture.

4. Evenly spread out the mixture on your lined baking sheet, then pop it in the oven for 15–20 minutes. Keep an eye on it to make sure it doesn't get TOO crispy.

5. Allow to cool on the baking sheet for 10–15 minutes.

**SEMI PRO TIP**: This concoction is the perfect little grab bag to give guests before they head home! Just grab some cute bags and some ribbon, and hand 'em out! Adults deserve more grab bags in their lives!

# ANCHOVY POPCORN

Okay, okay, okay. I can hear and feel your skepticism through these pages. I get it. It sounds weird and anchovies scare the hell out of people. But here's the thing: when they're cooked down in this melted butter/garlic situation, they literally disintegrate, and what's left behind is this beautiful rich savory umami flavor that will take your popcorn to the next level!

2 tbsp. butter

2 minced cloves of garlic

5 anchovies, chopped

1. In a saucepan, melt butter. Add the garlic and cook until aromatic, about 2 minutes, then add the anchovies. Keep stirring until they melt into the garlic butter mixture. It only takes a few minutes for them to completely disintegrate.

2. Pour over popcorn and stir to fully coat.

# CALAMARI WITH PEPPERONCINI, IF YA NASTY

*Serves 3–4*

I love me some calamari. Nine times out of ten, if we're out to dinner, we're ordering it. In fact, while in Maui for our honeymoon, my husband and I rode bikes around Kihei in search of the best calamari on the island. Sadly, I got too drunk to remember which place won the grand prize. (The grand prize was me taking my drunk ass back to the resort.) Anyway, making calamari at home is really easy. Something about frying up these little cutie squid rings is very satisfying and makes me feel like I'm the sensei of my kitchen. Throughout my journey of finding the best calamari, one thing I've grown to love is an added ingredient—be it lemon slices or jalapeño slices, sometimes the odd rogue fry will end up in your batch—but there's just something incredibly special that pepperoncini adds to the dish. Plus, I love the surprise of thinking it's a calamari ring. NOPE! Pepper, bitch! Anyways, this baby makes for a great appetizer when hosting a bunch of your favorite pals.

1 lb. calamari tubes and squids, tubes sliced into ½-inch rings, squid kept whole

1 cup pepperoncini rings

1 cup milk¾ cup flour

¾ cup corn starch

1 tsp. smoked paprika

2 tsp. salt

1 tsp. pepper

1 tsp. garlic powder

½ tsp. onion powderA couple inches worth of vegetable or canola oil

1. Rinse off your calamari. I recommend using fresh calamari if you can find it. Slice the calamari tubes into ½-in rings and leave the squid pieces whole. In a medium-sized bowl, cover the calamari and squid in the milk. Allow to sit 30 minutes to an hour. This is tenderizing the calamari, so you don't end up with chewy pieces.

2. Meanwhile, you can make your flour coating. Combine all of the dry ingredients and whisk together to fully combine. Set aside.

3. Once the calamari are ready to fry, get your oil heated. In a heavy-bottomed pot, a Dutch oven, or a deep fryer if you have one, add the oil and bring to 365 degrees.

4. Drain the calamari from the milk and add in the pepperoncini rings. Working in batches, coat the peppers and calamari in the flour mixture. Then, carefully add to the hot oil, remembering not to crowd the pot. Fry for about 3–4 minutes until golden brown and crispy. Repeat with remaining calamari and peppers.

5. Serve with lemon wedges and your favorite dipping sauce or this lemon dill aioli.

## LEMON DILL AIOLI

1 cup mayonnaise

1 tbsp. fresh dill, chopped

1 tsp. salt

½ tsp. pepper

1 tsp. garlic powder

zest of one lemon

juice of one lemon

Combine all ingredients. Keep chilled until ready to serve.

# COCONUT SHRIMP

*Serves 4–6*

Shrimp rolled around in some sweet coconut and then deep fried to golden perfection? Hell to the MF'ing yes! These are always gonna be a crowd pleaser, unless you're allergic to shellfish. In that case, do not make this. But if you're down with these critters from the sea, saddle up, partner.

16 oz. raw shrimp (21–25 jumbo shrimp)

½ cup all-purpose flour

½ cup panko

1 cup sweetened shredded coconut

2 large eggs

1 tbsp. Dijon mustard

canola oil or vegetable oil

1. If you're working with frozen shrimp, thaw them in a bowl of cold water. Remove the shells but leave the tails on.

2. In a Dutch oven or heavy pot, heat the oil to 325 degrees. You're going to need it to be a few inches deep. About 2 cups' worth should do it. Keep an eye on it with a deep fry/high temperature thermometer if you're not using a deep fryer. And remember to allow the heat to rise again between batches.

3. Set up your shrimp station! You'll need 3 bowls. Flour in one, eggs and Dijon mixed well in a second, and the panko/coconut mixture in the third.

4. Dry your shrimp with a paper towel or cloth. Holding onto the tails, begin to coat well in the flour, then transfer to the egg mixture, then the coconut mixture. Make sure they're completely coated. Carefully lower into the oil. Fry them for about 2–3 minutes per side. Transfer to a wire rack to cool.

5. Serve with a sweet chili dipping sauce!

# BEEF PATTIES

*Serves 6–8*

My childhood contained beef patties a plenty! I loved the frozen ones you could just pop in the microwave for 2 minutes and voila: spicy beefy flavor pocket. Unfortunately, they're hard to come across in my part of town, which is a complete and utter bummer. FRET NOT. I've learned how to make them from my very own domicile. Bless this book for making me not stress out when a recipe requires me to make dough. This flakey turmeric-and-curry-flavored dough comes together in a hot minute, and the beef mixture has SO much flavor. I feel like allspice doesn't get enough love. So, now we can get heavy handed with it in this recipe.

| | |
|---|---|
| 3 cups flour | 1 tbsp. allspice |
| 1 tsp. salt | 1 tsp. curry powder |
| 2 tsp. turmeric | 1 tsp. smoked paprika |
| 1 tsp. curry powder | 1 tsp. red pepper chili flakes |
| 1 cup cold unsalted butter, cut into cubes | 1 tsp. fresh pepper |
| 1 egg | 1 tsp. salt |
| 1 tsp. vinegar | 2 tbsp. soy sauce |
| ½ cup cold water | 1½ cups beef stock |
| | 2 tbsp. flour |
| | |
| 2 tbsp. olive oil | |
| 2 shallots, about 1 cup, diced | 1 egg |
| 5 garlic cloves, minced | 2 tbsp. water |
| 1½–2 lbs. ground beef (80/20 fat ratio) | |

1. Let's make some dough, shall we? In a food processor, add the flour, salt, turmeric, curry powder, and butter. Pulse until it's all incorporated and has the consistency of wet sand.

2. Transfer to a bowl or stand mixer with the hook attachment.

3. Whisk the egg and vinegar and add it to the dough. Slowly start adding the water and mix until a ball has formed. If the dough is too sticky, add a tablespoon of flour at a time until the dough isn't wet to the touch anymore. If it's too dry, add a tablespoon of water at a time until the dough comes together. Wrap in Saran Wrap and chill for about an hour.

4. In a large pan over medium heat, heat the olive oil and add the shallot and garlic, stirring often until soft and translucent.

5. Add the ground beef. Break it up into pieces and cook until browned most of the way through. Add the allspice, curry powder, smoked paprika, chili flakes, pepper, salt, and soy sauce. Stir to combine.

6. Now add the beef stock and bring to a simmer. Allow to reduce for about 5-8 minutes. Then sprinkle in the 2 tablespoons of flour. Cook about another 3 minutes until the sauce thickens. Allow to cool.

7. Preheat the oven to 375 degrees.

8. Remove the dough from the fridge and cut in half. Place half back in the fridge until you're ready to use it. On a lightly floured surface roll out the dough to about ⅛ inch thick. Cut circles out of the dough. You want them to be about 5 inches across. I don't have a cookie cutter that big, so I use a soup bowl and just cut around the edge with a sharp knife.

9. Fill the middle of the dough with about a tablespoon and a half of the beef. Whisk together the egg and water, and with a pastry brush or back of a spoon run it along the inside edge of the dough. Fold the dough in half to make the patty shape, half-moon style. Seal the edges together by pinching the dough. You can use a fork to seal the edges too. Plus, it looks pretty. Repeat with remaining dough and beef.

10. Add the patties to a lined baking sheet. Bake at 375 for 20–25 minutes until golden and flakey. Cool. Serve!

SEMI PRO TIP: These are great to keep in the freezer. Just pop them out when you're hungry, wrap the patty in a piece of paper towel, microwave for 1 minute, rotate, and heat for another 30 seconds.

# CHORIZO STUFFED MUSHROOMS

*Serves 6–8*

Get ready to have your sweet little mind blown! Mushroom caps brimming with spicy chorizo, topped with pepper jack cheese and breadcrumbs. You'll want to eat the entire plate yourself, which is 100% approved by me. Just let them cool a bit when you take them out of the oven or else your whole mouth will burn, and you won't taste anything delicious for a few days. Word from the wise.

| | |
|---|---|
| 12 medium to large brown mushrooms | ½ cup shredded pepper jack cheese |
| 6 oz. chorizo | ½ cup breadcrumbs |
| 1 tbsp. olive oil | 1 tbsp. butter, melted |
| 1 garlic clove, minced | |

1. Preheat your oven to 400 degrees.

2. Gently wipe your mushrooms with a damp cloth to remove any dirt. Remove the stems and then finely chop them. You only need to keep half of the stems, about ½ a cup.

3. Heat a medium-sized pan over medium-high heat. Remove the chorizo from its casing and begin to break it apart with the back of a wooden spoon in the pan. Add the mushroom stems and minced garlic. Cook through for about 5–8 minutes.

4. In a bowl, combine the melted butter, breadcrumbs, and shredded pepper jack cheese.

5. Place the mushroom caps upside down on a lined baking sheet. Stuff each cap with the chorizo mixture. They can only hold about a teaspoon or so each, but cram as much filling as you can into each one.

6. Top each mushroom with the breadcrumb-and-cheese mixture.

7. Bake in the oven 20–25 minutes until mushroom caps are cooked through and the cheese is bubbling.

8. Serve immediately, but don't burn your mouth...you guys know the drill!

# Salad, Soups & Sides

Every good meal deserves a kick-ass side. Every good side deserves to be a stand-alone meal. You are the creator of your own food destiny! Pair these up or have at them on their own. I promise these dudes will enter your regular rotation. And yes, pasta salad is a SALAD. Do not @ me.

"AFTER ALL THE TROUBLE YOU GO TO, YOU GET ABOUT AS MUCH ACTUAL 'FOOD' OUT OF EATING AN ARTICHOKE AS YOU WOULD FROM LICKING 30 OR 40 POSTAGE STAMPS."

—MISS PIGGY

BRUSCHETTA
SALAD

ANTiPASTi
PASTA SALAD

RED PEPPER/BELLOW/
GOAT CHEESE SALAD

# RED PEPPER/BELLO/GOAT CHEESE SALAD

*Serves 4*

Let me just say that I really love this salad! I am not one to get overly amped about a salad, but this one rings my freaking bell. Ring, ding, dong, y'all! Portobellos are the best fungus gift from the dirt, and the red pepper/goat cheese combo is heavenly. The creaminess from the goat cheese paired up with this salty tangy dressing makes my mouth oh-so-happy. The dressing is great served warm, as well as the veggies, so the heat from the dressing and veggies help to warm up the goat cheese, hence coating all of your spinach AND MAKING YOU HAPPY!

| | |
|---|---|
| 1 bag of fresh spinach (16 oz.) | ¼ cup low-sodium soy sauce |
| 8 oz. Portobellos (about 3 medium), sliced | 1 tbsp. sesame oil |
| 1 large red pepper, sliced | 2 tbsp. apple cider vinegar |
| 2 tbsp. olive oil | 2 tbsp. honey |
| 4 oz. goat cheese | 1 tbsp. mirin |
| salt | 1 tsp. fresh ginger, grated |
| pepper | 1 garlic clove, grated |

1. In a small saucepan, combine all dressing ingredients and bring to a simmer for about 5 minutes. Remove from heat.

2. In a sauté pan, over medium-high heat, add the olive oil, peppers, and mushrooms. Cook until tender, about 10–12 minutes. Salt and pepper to taste.

3. Distribute the spinach in the bowls, divide up the goat cheese, and top with the veggies and warm salad dressing.

# BRUSCHETTA SALAD

*Serves 4–6*

Alright, guys, let's call this what it is: a bread salad. Sue me! I'm just out here trying to spark joy. It's bread turned into buttery garlicky croutons and tossed with some shallot, basil, and marinated tomatoes. It's good as all hell. Add some cheese if you're feeling dangerous, maybe a fancy blue cheese or some parmesan chunks. Personally, I enjoy letting the tomatoes do the heavy lifting here.

| | |
|---|---|
| 1 loaf of crusty bread chopped into 1-inch cubes. About 5 cups. | 2 tbsp. olive oil |
| | ¼ tsp. salt |
| 3 tbsp. salted butter | ¼ tsp. pepper |
| 2 garlic cloves, minced | 1 shallot, finely chopped |
| 1 lb. ripe tomatoes on the vine, chopped into quarters | 1 tbsp. fresh basil, chopped |

1. Preheat the oven to 375 degrees.

2. In a large microwave-safe bowl, melt the butter. Toss the bread chunks and the minced garlic until fully coated. On a lined baking sheet, lay the bread out in an even layer. Bake for about 15–20 minutes, tossing every 5 minutes to make sure it's all browning up evenly.

3. Meanwhile, toss the tomatoes, olive oil, shallot, basil, and salt and pepper. Stir to totally combine. Keep in the fridge until you're ready to serve.

4. Toss the croutons and the tomato mixture and serve.

**SEMI PRO TIP:** I always find it best to mix this together about 10–15 minutes before I'm about to serve it. This way the tomatoes and bread can combine, and the bread soaks up the tomato juices without getting too soggy. Overall, the croutons hold up pretty well, but they're best when they're still on the crunchy side.

# ANTIPASTI PASTA SALAD

*Serves 6–8*

Oh yes! All of your favorite antipasti flavors mixed up and tossed over a nice twisty pasta—saltiness from the salami, pepperoni, and feta; acidity from the tomatoes and banana peppers; and sweet freshness from the basil in the pesto dressing. Definitely serve this dude cold!

16 oz. short pasta (I used farfalle)

3 cups tomatoes, diced

1 cup artichoke hearts, diced

½ cup banana peppers, diced

6 oz. feta cheese, crumbled

4 oz. salami, sliced into thin strips

4 oz. uncured pepperoni, sliced into thin strips

1 cup pesto (see page 39 for pesto recipe)

Cook the pasta until al dente, add in all other ingredients, and toss with the pesto sauce. Allow to cool for a few hours before serving. This dish is a DREAM the next day.

# PEACH GOAT CHEESE SALAD WITH CANDIED PECANS

*Serves 4–6*

This is the salad of the summer—fresh juicy peaches combined with the tartness of goat cheese and a nice friendly slap in the mouth from the spicy sweet pecans. These pecans can be done ahead of time and are awesome to have on hand in the pantry. I usually just end up snacking on them when they're in the house because they're freaking delicious!

| | |
|---|---|
| 2 cups pecans, whole or crushed | 5 cups baby spinach |
| ¼ cup powdered sugar | 4–5 large peaches, sliced |
| 2 tbsp. water | 4 oz. goat cheese |
| ½ tsp. cayenne | |
| 4–5 dashes hot sauce | ¾ cup olive oil |
| ¼ tsp. salt | ¼ cup apple cider vinegar |
| | ¼ cup honey |

1. Preheat oven to 350 degrees.

2. Mix together the powdered sugar, water, cayenne, hot sauce, and salt. In a bowl, toss to coat the pecans.

3. On a lined and greased baking sheet, spread out the pecans in an even layer and bake for 10–12 minutes. The pecans will become very fragrant when they're ready. Allow to cool.

4. For the dressing, add the oil, apple cider vinegar, and honey to a bowl and whisk together until fully combined.

5. Assemble the spinach, peaches, and goat cheese. Drizzle with about ¼ cup of the salad dressing, and top with a handful of the spicy sweet pecans.

**SEMI PRO TIP**: You can keep this dressing in the fridge, in a sealed container, for about 3 weeks.

# MANGO SALAD

*Serves 4*

Something magical happens when you combine these distinct flavors and let them marinate for a few hours in the fridge. It's light and fresh and works as a perfect side for my Peanut Butter and Jelly Chicken or Coconut Curry Red Snapper. Here ya go!

2 mangoes, diced

½ cup red onion, julienned

¼ cup fresh cilantro, chopped

1 tbsp. fresh lime juice

1 pinch of salt

a few grinds of the pepper mill

¼ tsp. red pepper chili flakes

¼ cup crushed peanuts

Combine the mango, red onion, lime juice, salt, pepper, and red pepper chili flakes. Stir to fully coat. Then top with the fresh cilantro. Allow to sit for at least 30 minutes in the fridge for the flavors to combine! Top with the crushed peanuts just before serving.

# HAPPY TUNA SALAD

*Serves 4–6*

This recipe isn't going to earn you a Michelin star rating in your kitchen, BUT this is the kinda "makes you happy, always a pleasure to have in the fridge, rousing success if you bring it to a BBQ or picnic" type of dish. Do people still picnic? I really romanticize the idea of going on a picnic with a basket and blanket and all that shit. If I did, I would definitely pack this happy camper, along with an ice pack and some champagne. The point is, you will make a lot of people very happy with this dish. She's not trying too hard, and she always brings her *A* game with a great attitude. Best served cold.

1 box of elbow macaroni (16 oz.)

1 large green pepper, diced

¼ red onion, finely chopped

½ tsp. salt

½ tsp. pepper

¼ tsp. cayenne

1 cup mayonnaise

2 cans drained tuna (5 oz. each)

1. In a medium-sized pot, bring water to a boil. Season with salt. We like salt. Add in the macaroni or whatever pasta you decide to use, and cook based on box instructions until al dente. About 7–8 minutes.

2. MEANWHILE in chop-land...dice up your green pepper and onion.

3. Once the pasta is cooked to al dente, drain and add to a large bowl for all the mixin' and fixin's. Add in the mayo and coat the pasta while it's hot. Add the remaining ingredients and mix together well. Salt and pepper to taste.

4. Pop this little honey in the fridge and go nuts after it's perfectly chilled.

# NO NEW FRIENDS CAESAR SALAD

*Serves 4–6*

I love bold tastes so much that I sometimes wonder if there's something wrong with my palate. Give me all of the garlic. If you're the kind of person that doesn't want to mess around with egg yolk and anchovies, then please pass this book along to a friend that's willing to live life walking into a room tongue-first. This Caesar salad dressing is one my mom would make for us when my brother and I lived at home. I've always loved it, but it will give you garlic breath for around 48 hours. This could also be called the Marriage Caesar, because this ain't no first-date recipe. Only eat with a trusted group of friends that already know your secrets, because I wouldn't recommend trying to whisper anything important to anyone with this garlic breath. That being said, it's SO delicious. AND GARLIC IS GOOD FOR YOUR HEALTH! With the addition of homemade croutons and crispy bacon bits, bend me over and call me Bobby Flay.

16 oz romaine lettuce

## DRESSING

2 anchovies

3 cloves of garlic

½ tsp. salt

½ tsp. pepper

1 tbsp. Worcestershire sauce

1 tbsp. coarse Dijon mustard

1 juice of whole lemon

½ lemon rind

¼ cup fresh grated parmesan

½ cup olive oil

1. In either a blender or mortar and pestle (if you want to feel medieval AF) combine the anchovies, garlic, salt, and pepper and grind that good good up.

2. Add in the Worcestershire sauce, Dijon, the lemon juice, and the egg yolk. MIX IT UP. GET IN THERE.

3. Add the olive oil, slowly to emulsify. Once everything is in there and mixed up well, add in the parmesan.

4. Give her a taste and then add any extra salt and pepper.

## BACON

- 1/2 lb. of bacon

1. Cut the bacon into 1-inch slices and crisp in a pan over medium high heat. About 5–8 minutes.

2. Remove from the pan and allow to cool on a plate lined with paper towel to collect the excess grease.

## CROUTONS

- leftover baguette, cut into cubes—2 cups approx. (If you have a loaf of bread that's on its way out—I had a French baguette on my counter, so I used that.)

- 2 tbsp. butter
- 2 tbsp. olive oil
- salt
- pepper
- garlic powder

Preheat oven to 375 degrees. Add your bread cubes to a large bowl. Melt the butter and add in the olive oil. Now toss the bread and the butter-oil mixture together. Give a good sprinkle with salt, pepper, and garlic powder. Again, get creative here, these are just guidelines. You can flavor your croutons any way your little heart desires. On a lined baking sheet, spread out the bread in an even layer, and bake for about 15–20 minutes until golden brown. Toss about halfway through for even browning of the croutons.

## ASSEMBLE!

Rinse your romaine lettuce so we don't all get whatever disease romaine might be carrying, then dry it off. Drizzle on the dressing, then add the croutons, bacon, and some more parmesan to top. A fresh squeeze of lemon, and then GO IN.

**SEMI PRO TIP**: Feel free to experiment with adding different flavors to your bacon. Add some garlic to the bacon when cooking it, or brown sugar, or rosemary. The bacon is your oyster.

# FRESH PRETZELS WITH BEER CHEESE SOUP

*Serves 4–6*

Since we've all gathered here to be a tad indulgent, and occasionally experimental, I thought this beer cheese soup fit the bill quite nicely. If you have a certain beer on deck that you want to try, you have my full support. To my taste, I say a lager or blonde beer is the best move. I was basic AF the first time I made this and used Miller Lite because it's what was in the fridge…also I just like Miller Lite. SUE ME! 90 calories in a beer?! Yes, stock my fridge, thankyouverymuch. For the cheese, I use sharp cheddar. The pretzels and this soup go hand in hand. These pretzels are seriously so easy to make and have a huge payoff in your yap.

## PRETZELS

| | |
|---|---|
| 1½ cups warm water | 3 tbsp. melted butter |
| 1 tbsp. sugar | 2 eggs |
| 1 tbsp. salt | 3 tbsp. water |
| 1 packet yeast | flakey salt (Maldon is my go-to) |
| 3½ cups flour | ¼ cup baking soda |

1. In a large mixing bowl combine the warm water, salt, and sugar. Mix to dissolve the sugar and salt. Add the yeast. Give it a quick little stir, and let it sit until it starts to look a little foamy and creamy, about 5 minutes.

2. Add the flour and 2 tablespoons of the melted butter to the yeast mixture and stir to combine into a beautiful round ball of pretzel dough. If the dough still feels too sticky, add a tablespoon of flour until the dough is no longer sticking to your fingers. Remove the dough from the bowl. Use the other tablespoon of melted butter to grease the bowl, then put the dough back in the bowl. Cover with Saran Wrap and leave in a warm spot for an hour. I leave mine on my kitchen counter.

3. Preheat your oven to 450.

4. Bring a medium pot of water to a boil, add in the ¼ cup of baking soda.

5. Mix your eggs and water in a bowl. You're going to brush the tops of the pretzels before you pop 'em in the oven.

6. Once your dough has risen, cut the dough ball in half. Then cut each half into 4 equal-ish pieces. Roll each piece into a long skinny rope, then fold into the perfect pretzel shape! Working with one at a time, carefully place in the boiling water and cook 30–40 seconds a side before removing with a slotted spoon. Place the boiled pretzel onto a parchment-lined baking sheet.

7. Brush with the egg wash and sprinkle with the flakey salt. Repeat with all 8 pretzels. Put them in the oven for 10–15 minutes until golden brown on top. Your house now smells amazing.

## BEER CHEESE SOUP

4 carrots, diced

2 celery stalks, diced

1 large yellow onion, diced

2 garlic cloves, minced

1 serrano pepper, diced—seeds removed (Unless you want some extra spice in your life!)

1 tbsp. olive oil

1 tsp. cayenne

½ tsp. salt

½ tsp. pepper

6 tbsp. butter

⅓ cup flour

3 cups low-sodium chicken stock

2 cups blonde beer

4 cups whole milk or half and half

1½ tbsp. Dijon mustard

1 tbsp. Worcestershire sauce

1 tsp. dry mustard

8 cups shredded sharp cheddar cheese.

## SLURRY

½ cup chicken broth

2 tbsp. flour

1. In a large heavy pot, heat the olive oil, then add the carrots, celery, onion, and garlic and cook until they start to soften. About 5 minutes. Add in the serrano pepper, cayenne, salt, and pepper. Coat all the veggies. Add the butter and melt it down. Sprinkle on the flour and coat the veggies again. Cook for about 3 minutes until the flour is fully incorporated and starts to get a really delicious nutty smell. Then add the chicken stock and the beer and return to a simmer. Using an immersion blender, slowly start to blend the stock to a smoother consistency. Now slowly add the milk and continue to whisk to combine. Working slowly helps it combine. Add the Dijon, Worcestershire sauce, and dry mustard. Then add the real star of the dish—ALL DAT CHEESE. Keep whisking until the cheese is completely melted into the sauce.

2. To thicken the soup, create a slurry: whisk together ½ cup of chicken broth and 2 tbsp. of flour. Slowly mix it into the soup until it's completely blended.

**SEMI PRO TIP:** *Get creative with the pretzels! Instead of the flakey salt, you could do everything bagel mix, garlic powder, cheese, endless options! You could even do cinnamon sugar for those sweet-tooth cravings!*

# CORN SOUP

*Serves 6–8*

I have only been to Japan once, for like two and a half days, and it rocked my freaking world. It was easily my favorite trip of my life. I'm incredibly lucky that I get to travel so much for work and see the world, relentlessly shoving foods in my mouth from city to city, state to state, and continent to continent. While in Japan, I had to make the most of my time because it was so short. I bopped around Harajuku, did karaoke, went to a hedgehog café, and per my husband's insistence, we HAD to buy a bunch of wild snacks from the 7-Eleven around the corner—noodle sandwiches, whipped cream sandwiches, butter and soy chips, hot coffee and tea in cans. It was incredible! Our hotel had breakfast laid out every morning. Let me tell you, the Japanese are down with soup for breakfast, which is my dream! All I ever want is a broth or soup, especially after I've gone hard on the lemon sours the night before. So, this was my first experience of corn soup. It's like liquid corn on the cob. Of course, I needed to make my own once I returned stateside.

| | |
|---|---|
| 5 tbsp. unsalted butter | 2½ tbsp. flour |
| 1 cup shallots, chopped | 1 tsp. salt |
| 1 garlic clove, minced | ¼ tsp. pepper |
| 6 corn cobs | |
| 6 cups low-sodium chicken stock | fine mesh sieve |
| 1 cup half and half | blender |

1. In a large pot, melt the butter, then add the shallots and garlic. Cook over medium/high heat until soft, about 5–8 minutes.

2. Meanwhile, take your corn cobs and start cutting off the corn kernels with a sharp knife. Keep the corn spines. Are they called spines? The corn body, or whatever. Keep those! You're gonna add them to the stock for some deep corn flavor!

3. Once the shallot/garlic combo is nice and soft, add in the kernels and heat through, about 5 minutes. Add the chicken stock and the corn spines and bring to a simmer. Allow to simmer for about 20 minutes, then remove and discard the corn spines.

4. Let the soup cool a bit before transferring to a blender. No need to go scalding yourself. Unless you're using an immersion blender; in that case have at it right away and blend until smooth. If you're using a traditional blender, carefully add to the blender in batches and puree until smooth.

5. Now, over a large bowl, work the soup through a fine mesh sieve to get rid of any chunks from the corn, shallots, and garlic.

6. Once you're left with the creamy soup, pour that baby back into the pot you were cooking in and return to a simmer.

7. In a separate bowl, whisk the half and half with the flour and slowly pour it into the soup. It will begin to thicken up. Add the salt and pepper and serve with some buttery croutons on top.

# JALAPEÑO POPPER MAC 'N' CHEESE

*Serves 8–10*

I couldn't write a cookbook and NOT have a mac 'n' cheese recipe. I'm neither a chef nor a legit writer, so the least I can do is acknowledge the essentials. It goes without saying that mac 'n' cheese is just that—essential service. So, here's everyone's favorite late-night bar snack jam-packed into a bubbly, cheesy, bread-crumb-topping best friendship. These two go together like lipstick and leopard print.

¼ cup flour

½ stick butter (4 tbsp.)

2 cups half and half

8 oz. cream cheese

2 cups Manchego cheese, shredded

4 cups white cheddar cheese

2 cups 2% milk

3 jalapeños, seeds removed and diced

1 lb. macaroni noodles

½ tsp. salt

½ tsp. pepper

½ lb. bacon, diced

½ cup Manchego cheese, shredded

½ cup white cheddar, shredded

¾ cup breadcrumbs

2 tbsp. butter, melted

1. Preheat oven to 375 degrees.

2. Bring a large pot of salted water to a boil and cook the macaroni to just under al dente, about 2 minutes earlier than the directions on the box. Drain and set aside. The noodles will continue to cook in the oven. We don't want them to get all mushy.

3. In the large pot, melt the half stick of butter and whisk in the flour. Cook for a few minutes and the flour will get a nice nutty smell. Add the half and half and it will begin to thicken. Add the cream cheese and stir until melted. Start to add in the cheese until just melted. Then slowly add in the 2% milk. Stir to fully combine and allow to simmer until thickened back up. Salt and pepper to taste. Add in the jalapeños and the macaroni and stir until it's all completely combined.

4. In a frying pan, crisp the ½ lb. of bacon. About 8–10 minutes. Drain on a paper towel and run a knife through it to coarsely chop it.

5. In a microwave safe bowl, melt the 2 tbsp. of butter. Add the breadcrumbs and mix together into a sand-like texture.

6. In a 9x13 baking dish, add the mac 'n' cheese situation. Evenly top with the crumbled bacon, the ½ cup of Manchego, ½ cup of white cheddar, and the breadcrumbs.

7. Bake at 375 for about 20–25 minutes until bubbling and the breadcrumbs are a golden brown and crispy.

# HAWAIIAN FRIED RICE

*Serves 6–8*

Don't freak out over the SPAM! This polarizing greasy ham delight deserves your love, attention, and respect. I'm pretty sure people who say they hate SPAM have never actually tried it. I would know. I used to be one of them. Give SPAM a chance. Make America SPAM again! The good crisp in this recipe truly changes the SPAM game. Anyways, if I haven't sold you yet, fine; use cubed ham, dork. My one other tidbit here is using leftover rice or cooking the rice the day before. It's going to be more dried out, avoiding any gooping together.

| | |
|---|---|
| 1 12 oz. can SPAM, cut into cubes | 3 cups cooked white rice (Preferably leftover rice. Its dryness helps with the texture.) |
| 1 cup onion, diced | |
| ½ cup green pepper, diced | 3 tbsp. low-sodium soy sauce |
| 1 cup pineapple, diced, juices drained | 2 large eggs |
| | 2 tbsp. olive oil |

1. In your largest frying pan, heat 1 tbsp. olive oil and add the cubed SPAM, or ham. Cook it up over medium high heat until it's nice and crispy! About 8–10 minutes. Crispy SPAM is good SPAM. Remove from the pan and set aside.

2. Heat remaining tablespoon of olive oil, add the onion and green pepper to the pan over medium heat, cook through until soft, about 5–8 minutes. Meanwhile crack your eggs into a bowl and give them a quick whisk. Add them to the pan and cook through. Add the rice and mix everything together. Add the SPAM into the rice party, followed by the soy sauce and pineapple. Stir the rice all together until it's fully coated in the soy sauce. Cue up the Mai Tais and luau/BBQ playlist.

# COCONUT RICE

*Serves 4–6*

Coconut rice is the most exceptional rice. It's slightly on the sweet side, and combined with the insanely creamy texture, it really kicks meals up a notch, especially when we're talking combining coconut rice with some sort of curry situation. My mouth gets happy just thinking about it.

- 1 can sweetened coconut milk
- ½ cup water
- 1 cup jasmine rice

This is super easy. Literally, put all of the ingredients in a medium pot, throw on the lid, and bring to a simmer, then reduce heat to medium-low. Careful it doesn't boil over; the coconut milk can bubble up very quickly. So just keep it on low once it begins to simmer. Check around the 12-minute mark. Once the liquid has been absorbed and the rice is cooked through, fluff it with a fork and welcome yourself to coconut rice heaven.

# HERB INFUSED MASHED POTATOES

*Serves 8–10*

I LOVE THESE SO DAMN MUCH. Mashed potatoes with gravy would quite possibly be on my death row menu. They're buttery, creamy, and fluffy. Infusing the milk with herbs packs a hell of a punch. On my quest to making the best mashed potatoes imaginable, I perused A LOT of mashed potato literature, and it seems, according to many reputable potato sites, that a combination of russet and Yukon Gold potatoes is how we achieve ultimate success. I can confirm that this did not disappoint. These are my favorite side dish, and I'll probably make them at every holiday until I croak.

| | |
|---|---|
| 3 lbs. russet potatoes | bunch of thyme |
| 3 lbs. Yukon Gold potatoes | bunch of rosemary |
| 1½ cups whole milk | 1 tsp. salt |
| 1 stick unsalted butter (8 tbsp.) | 1 tsp. white pepper |
| 2 garlic cloves, smashed with the side of a knife | |

1. I always peel my potatoes because I use a potato ricer for my mashed potatoes. If you're using a potato masher, leave the skins on if you want that added texture.

2. Peel the potatoes and cut into even-sized cubes. Fill a large pot with the potatoes and cold water. Bring to a boil. Allow to cook until a knife can easily be inserted into the potatoes. About 18-20 minutes.

3. While the potatoes are cooking, prepare the infused milk. Over medium heat, bring the milk to a simmer and add the garlic, thyme, and rosemary. About 3 sprigs of each. Allow to simmer about 5 minutes on low. Remove the garlic and herbs.

4. When the potatoes are soft, drain them. Over the same large pot, put all of the potatoes through the ricer. Add the butter by the tablespoon and stir until melted. Slowly add the milk by the ½ cup. Stir to combine and salt and pepper to taste.

# Sandos

As a carb enthusiast, I'll happily eat just about anything that finds itself crammed between two slices of bread. No need for plates or cutlery, this is just about you and the sandwich, held in a gentle but firm, authoritative grasp in your hard-working hands. Grill it, squish it, fry it; the options are endless, so here's a few more to add to your sandwich playbook.

"I ORDERED A CLUB SANDWICH, BUT I'M NOT EVEN A MEMBER. 'I LIKE MY SANDWICHES WITH THREE PIECES OF BREAD.' 'WELL, SO DO I!' 'THEN LET'S FORM A CLUB.' 'OKAY, BUT WE NEED SOME MORE STIPULATIONS. INSTEAD OF CUTTING THE SANDWICH ONCE, LET'S CUT IT AGAIN. YES, FOUR TRIANGLES, ARRANGED IN A CIRCLE, AND IN THE MIDDLE, WE WILL DUMP CHIPS.' 'HOW DO YOU FEEL ABOUT FRILLY TOOTHPICKS?' 'I'M FOR 'EM!' 'WELL, THIS CLUB IS FORMED.'"

— MITCH HEDBERG, MITCH ALL TOGETHER

# FRENCH ONION SOUP GRILLED CHEESE

*Serves 1*

Oh yeah, you read that right. French onion soup was a recipe I wanted to add to this lovely culinary novel, which you are currently holding, but that seemed a little too straightforward for me, so BLAM-MO…I made that salty, oniony delight into a freaking sandwich. The best part of French onion soup is the bread and the cheese anyways, am I right? So, let's embark on a taste-bud-provoking treat, perfect for literally any time of the day. The caramelized onions keep in the fridge covered for a week.

2 yellow onions, sliced

4 tbsp. salted butter

2 tbsp. flour

3/4 cup beef broth

salt and pepper to taste

1.  CARAMELIZE THE ONIONS, making them a la French onion soup. In a Dutch oven, or a pan with tall sides (so the onions don't end up all over your stovetop), heat over medium-low heat and add the butter. Then start adding in the onions; you can start to cook them in batches and once they start to soften you can create more space in the pan for more onion-y goodness. This is a slooooowwwwwwwwww-ass process, so make sure you have a goblet of wine nearby to keep you occupied. Spin some jams by hitting up one of my playlists. Keep stirring the onions every few minutes. If they start browning too fast, lower the temperate. If the pan starts to get dry, add in a knob of butter. Just keep an eye on these suckers. After about 15–20 minutes they start to enter Caramelized Onion Land, but they're still not quite there. After about another 15–20 you should be closing in on the sweet spot.

2.  **Use these pictures as reference for the depth of color you're looking for. It's a truly magical moment to finally achieve. Pour yourself more wine.

3.  Now to give the real nod to the French onion soup. Add in ½ cup of beef broth (reserve ¼ of the broth for the slurry) and bring it to a simmer. Now take the ¼ cup of the beef broth that's been set aside to make your slurry; add 1 tbsp. of flour, and mix it well to get rid of any lumps. Slowly add the slurry to the onions-and-broth mixture. It will start to thicken almost immediately.

4.  Remove from heat and then salt and pepper to taste.

½ cup Gruyère cheese, grated

½ cup Swiss cheese, grated

¼ cup parmesan, grated

1 tbsp. butter

2 slices of sourdough bread for each sandwich you plan on grilling

1. TIME TO ASSEMBLE THIS SON OF A B! Like any other grilled cheese you've created before, you gotta butter the outside of the bread. Don't be shy. Then give a sprinkle of that parmesan to the buttered bread. It's gonna be on the outside of the bread so you get that crunchy-heavenly-burnt-cheese-thing happening. It's decadent.

2. With your pan on medium heat, add the first slice of buttered/parm bread to the pan, buttered side down. Then sprinkle on a mixture of the cheese blend. Spread about 2 tablespoons of the onion concoction on top of the cheese. Now another heavy-handed helping of the cheese mixture. Then top off with the remaining cheesy/buttery slice of bread. It should look like a sandwich now.

3. Flip the sandwich after about 3 minutes to grill up the opposite side. Let it cook another 3 minutes. If the cheese isn't melted to your desired meltyness, put a lid on the pan and drop the heat to avoid burning.

4. Once the cheese is melted and the bread is grilled through, you've got yourself a damn French Onion Soup Grilled Cheese. Cut in half whichever way your little heart desires. No one here is judging you, but diagonal is the only real way to cut a sandwich, if you have any self-respect.

**SEMI PRO TIP**: I find slow cooking things to be the most therapeutic thing. Put on some jams, give yourself a heavy pour of your libation of choice and take your time. Slow 'n' low. It's worth it in the end. You can use any leftover onions in eggs, salads, rice dishes, and pastas. They're great to have on hand to give a dish a little extra love.

# FISH 'N' CHIPS SANDWICH

*Serves 6*

My mom used to take us to this old fish and chips joint just outside of Toronto called Duckworth's. You know the kind, at least I hope you do. I'm talking thick-cut fries, salty buttery flakey fish, creamy coleslaw, and a side of gravy served wrapped in page 6 of the newspaper. An oily, greasy delight. Top with a strong dousing of malt vinegar and a ton of salt. (One day I will die from salt consumption. I know this. Just know I lived both happy and bloated.)

Anyways, while I was conjuring up ideas of how I wanted to present food to you lovely people, I was on the fence as to whether to do a fried chicken or fried fish sandwich. Given that I think the fried fish sandwich is the lost voice of our generation, I'm bringing mother effing fish sticks and fish and chips back, babaaaayyyyyy.

I wanted to do a play on fish and chips but sandwich style. Instead of fries, I subbed in a potato roll. And to make up for the absence of malt-vinegar-soaked fries, I made a malt vinegar aioli!

## MALT VINEGAR AIOLI

1 cup mayonnaise

¼ cup malt vinegar

1 garlic clove, finely chopped or grated

1 tablespoon Dijon mustard

salt and pepper to taste

## FISHIES

- 3 cod filets, cut in half to fit the sandwich
- canola oil/vegetable oil
- 1 cup light beer (I used Kirin Light, but whatever suits ya.)
- ¼ cup cornstarch
- ¾ cup all-purpose flour
- 1 tbsp. baking powder
- 1 egg
- salt
- pepper
- 1 tsp. smoked paprika
- 6 potato rolls

## COLESLAW

- 14 oz. bag of shredded cabbage
- ½ cup mayo
- 1 tbsp. white vinegar
- 1 tbsp. white sugar
- ¼ tsp. salt
- ½ tsp. pepper

1. Make the aioli first so the flavors can hang out and get acquainted with one another while the frying is happening. Just mix together all the ingredients and turn your attention to the fish! Let the aioli hang in the fridge.

2. Assemble the coleslaw. Like the aioli, it can hang out and do its coleslaw thing while you prepare this heavenly sandwich. I like to mix together the mayo, vinegar, and sugar in one larger bowl, and then just add the shredded cabbage to the coleslaw dressing. Toss it around to evenly cover all the cabbage!

## NOW THE FISHIES!

1. Pour enough oil into your Dutch oven to have about 2 inches deep. Heat oil to 365 degrees.

2. While oil is heating: pat down the fish and hit it with a little salt 'n' peps. Then, in a medium bowl, you'll have a mixture of cornstarch, AP flour, baking powder, salt, pepper, and paprika. Mix together the dry ingredients. Then add the egg to the dry ingredients and slowly start to mix the beer into the batter. Don't go wild because you wanna save those bubbles!

3. Dredge your fish fillets into the batter and drop immediately into the hot oil in your Dutch oven. Fry until golden brown on both sides. About 3–4 minutes per side. Once the batter turns a lovely crunchy golden color, you'll be in business.

4. Remove the fish from the fryer and place on a wire rack to cool. Keep an eye on the temperature of the oil after you've started adding the fillets. Make sure the heat returns to 365 before frying up the next fishy.

## TIME TO ASSEMBLE!

1. Toss the potato rolls, sliced in half and buttered, into the oven under broil to toast them golden brown. It happens quick, so don't walk away and start a new task! Keep an eye on your bread, sis!

2. Slap on a nice layer of the malt vinegar aioli on both cut sides of the bread, add your fish fillet, then a healthy mound of coleslaw. Top off your sando with the other slice of bread. You know, normal sandwich style. I don't even know why I'm describing the assembly. YOU KNOW HOW TO MAKE A SANDWICH. I DON'T KNOW HOW TO WRITE A COOKBOOK. DO I STILL NEED TO WRITE THESE THINGS?

3. Anyhoo, pip pip. Enjoy your fish 'n' chips sandwich more than Meghan Markle enjoyed being a PRINCESS.

# SMOOSH BURGERS

*Serves 6*

In the age-old debate of "In-N-Out vs. Shake Shack," I'd like to formally announce that my family is FIRMLY behind Shake Shack. These are the BEST fast-food burgers you can get your filthy paws on. But like any woman worth her salt, I like to give all of my favorite takeout meals a run for their money in the comfort of my own home. Hence, I present to you, your very own Shake Shack-style smashed burger. Yeah, I know people freak out when you press the juices out of a burger, but in this case the fat you smash down gives you the beautiful salty crispy edges on that burg. So, when you're buying your ground beef, make sure that you get the 80/20 lean-to-fat ratio. Your lean meat is not invited to this party. Also, I highly recommend this recipe with a cast-iron skillet. Using the skillet on the BBQ is one of my favorite tricks to keep that grill flavor in the burger, but you can totally do these on the stove top.

## THE SAUCE

- ½ cup mayonnaise
- ¼ cup ketchup
- ¼ cup finely chopped onions
- ¼ cup finely chopped dill pickles

Combine all of the ingredients and set aside in the fridge.

## THE BURGERS

- 1½–2 lbs. 80/20 ground beef
- 1 tsp. salt + more for seasoning
- ½ tsp. pepper
- Single-sliced cheese (optional)
- Burger buns

1. Turn on your grill (or stove top) and place your skillet on the grill to get it screaming hot.

2. In a large bowl, combine the meat, salt, and pepper. Get your hands in there and combine it well and then form 6 equal-sized balls. About a good palm full. Leave in balls; the smashing happens after. Sprinkle the top of each ball with a pinch of salt. Place the balls on your skillet—you want to hear that music-to-your-ears "sear" sound right away because the skillet is so hot. With the back of a metal spatula, smash your burger down to about 1 inch thick. Allow to cook about 2–3 minutes with the BBQ lid down. Flip to the other side, smash down again. Add your cheese if you're using it and cook another 2–3 minutes. Remove from the heat and then build your burgers starting with a healthy layer of the sauce! GO IN!

# THE LAMB JAM (A.K.A. THE LAMBURGER)

*Serves 4*

Ground lamb is a delightful meat. I consider it under-loved and under-appreciated, and I think it's about damn time that it gets its moment in the sun. I tinkered with this recipe while in quarantine for the COVID-19 pandemic. If you recall, getting your hands on some ground beef during this time was near impossible, so it forced me to go a little out of my comfort zone and try different meats. It was either that orrrrrrr just cram mac and cheese down my yap. So, I had some ground lamb and I really wanted to give this bad boy a little Greek spin. While I am not Greek, I thoroughly enjoy time spent on the Danforth in Toronto during Taste of the Danforth (mostly all delicious Greek food), plus I used to live in Astoria, Queens, a predominantly Greek neighborhood…so basically through osmosis I'm an authority on the subject. Kinda. What I mean by that is I like tzatziki, dolma, and baklava a lot.

## FOR THE TZATZIKI

I'd try to make this in advance, only due to having to drain the cucumber. But if you're in a pinch, you'll be fine. This will leave you plenty of tzatziki left over, so get out some crispy pitas later!

- 1½ cups cucumber, grated and strained. Use cheesecloth, a sieve, or a clean kitchen towel. Get out as much of the water from the cucumber as you can.

- 2 cups full-fat Greek yogurt

- 2 medium-sized garlic cloves, minced

- juice of half a lemon

- 1 tsp. grated lemon zest

- 1 tbsp. fresh dill, finely chopped

- ½ tsp. salt

- a few cracks of the peppermill

While you are draining the water from your cucumber, take the minced garlic and add it to the Greek yogurt to let those flavors start to come together and also take a bit of the edge off that raw garlic. Then add the lemon juice, lemon rind, salt, pepper, and dill. Stir to combine. Then take your grated cucumber and add it to the yogurt situation. Stir to combine. And *OPA!* Smash a plate and take a shot of ouzo. It's time for the burgers!

## FOR THE PATTIES

This makes 4. Double it up if you have more mouths to feed.

| | |
|---|---|
| 1 tbsp. olive oil | ¼ tsp. pepper |
| 1 lb. ground lamb | ½ tsp. salt |
| 1 garlic clove, minced | 2 sprigs of rosemary, finely chopped |

1. Combine all ingredients, except the olive oil, until thoroughly incorporated. Divide equally and roll into patties. Leave a small indent in the middle to help it keep its shape once you start cooking.

2. In a large frying pan, heat the oil over medium-high heat, then proceed to cook the patties about 3–4 minutes per side.

## FOR THE ASSEMBLY

Sliced tomato

Thinly sliced onion

Burger buns

ASSEMBLE THIS BURG!

1. Toast up your buns in the oven! Using the broiler, place your buns on a baking sheet and place them under the broiler for a few minutes, until nice and golden brown. Keep an eye on them—the broiler can sneak up on you really quick and scorch your buns.

2. Place a nice thick layer of the tzatziki on the bottom bun, then the lamb patty, tomato, and onion. DONE!

# BÁNH MÌ PANINI

*Serves 6*

All of the mouth-watering sweet-salty flavors of the Vietnamese sandwich, but pressed and grilled! Oh, and I added cheese because no harm has ever come from adding cheese, unless you're lactose intolerant. In that case, ditch the cheese for yours and your loved one's sake. I crave bánh mì sandwiches all the time, but my favorite local Vietnamese restaurant doesn't have them on the menu, so I improvised a simple marinade on thinly sliced pork loin combined with a quick pickling to carrots, radish, and serrano pepper. If pickling some veggies seems like a tall order to you…I pinky promise that it's so much easier than you think, and ready in about 10 minutes.

## PICKLED VEGGIES

- 1 cup carrots, finely sliced
- 1 cup radishes, finely sliced
- 2 serrano peppers, seeds removed, diced
- ½ cup rice wine vinegar
- 1 tbsp. sugar
- 2 tsp. salt

1. For the quick pickling of the veggies, combine the rice wine vinegar, sugar, and salt. Add the carrots, radish, and serrano pepper. Allow them to hang in the vinegar bath for about 10 minutes. You want them to stay crispy! Ain't no one got time for soggy pickles!

# PORK

- 2-3 lb. pork loin
- ½ cup hoisin sauce
- 1 garlic clove, minced
- ¼ cup rice wine vinegar
- 2 tbsp. fish sauce
- ¼ tsp. sesame oil

1. I read a tip somewhere to put your pork loin in the freezer for about 15–20 minutes because it makes it so much easier to thinly slice. They weren't lying! So, let your pork hang in there while you prepare yourthe marinade.

2. In a bowl combine the hoisin sauce, garlic, rice wine vinegar, fish sauce, and sesame oil. Stir well to combine.

3. Begin to slice your pork as thinly as you can. I like to cut mine on a bias—on an angle—so that I end up with some longer slices of the pork. Add the pork to the marinade, toss to coat evenly, and allow to sit for at least 30 minutes.

4. Heat a pan over medium-high heat. In batches, begin to cook the pork. You don't want to crowd the pan, but the pork will cook pretty quickly. Once cooked all the way through, about 5–6 minutes, transfer to a plate and begin the next batch.

- 12 slices white bread

- 12 slices Swiss cheese

- fresh cilantro bunch

- fresh basil

1. Once all the pork is cooked, it's time to assemble the sandwiches!

2. Butter one side of each bread slice. Add cheese to both sandwich slices. Build the pork, pickled vegetables, and a good heap of cilantro and basil.

3. On a heated panini press, add the sandwiches, and cook until the bread is golden brown and crispy and the cheese has melted. Slice in half and go to town!

**SEMI PRO TIP**: The pork can be prepared and marinated the night before. Makes life much easier when you have hungry guests looming around in the kitchen. Just pop it out of the fridge and go. It's cooked all the way through so quickly because of the thin slices. Sandwiches will be on the table in no time!

If you don't have a panini press, no problem! Just pre-heat a pan and use something as a weight to press the sandwich. Another pan, a heavy plate, or a dish will do the trick!

# PULLED MUSHROOM SANDWICHES

*Serves 6*

I am not a vegetarian, but I've dabbled for a month or so here and there, and mushrooms were my saving grace for making things seem meaty. The texture of the portobello combined with a tangy BBQ sauce makes this a great summertime staple. And they're so easy to pull together. Basically, it's just making the BBQ sauce. Hey, you can obviously skip that entirely and just use a store-bought one if you prefer, but since I'm writing a whole freaking cookbook, I figured I better have a BBQ sauce recipe to go with this mushroom number. Plus, you can make the sauce ahead of time and store it in the fridge for a few weeks.

| | |
|---|---|
| 6 large portobello mushrooms | Coleslaw |
| 1–1½ cups BBQ sauce | Dill pickles to top |
| 6 hamburger buns | |

## BBQ SAUCE

| | |
|---|---|
| 1 (20 oz.) bottle of ketchup | ¼ tsp. dry mustard |
| ¼ cup apple cider vinegar | ½ tsp. smoked paprika |
| 1 tbsp. Worcestershire sauce | ½ tsp. salt |
| ¼ cup brown sugar | ¼ tsp. pepper |
| ½ tsp. onion powder | 1 tbsp. honey |
| 1 tsp. garlic powder | a few dashes hot sauce |

Let's get the BBQ sauce started. In a medium saucepan, combine all ingredients until fully...um...combined. Allow to simmer for about 5–8 minutes. You can use this immediately or store in your fridge for future BBQ sauce needs.

## COLESLAW

| | |
|---|---|
| 14 oz. bag of shredded cabbage | 1 tbsp. white sugar |
| ½ cup mayo | ¼ tsp. salt |
| 1 tbsp. white vinegar | ½ tsp. pepper |

Just like the coleslaw in the Fish 'N' Chips Sandwich, I like to mix together the mayo, vinegar, sugar, salt, and pepper in one larger bowl, and then just add the shredded cabbage to that coleslaw dressing. Toss it around to evenly cover all the cabbage!

## FOR THE PULLED MUSHROOM MAGIC

1. Preheat oven to 425 degrees.

2. On a lined baking sheet, brush both sides of the mushrooms with a heavy-handed helping of BBQ sauce. Bake 20–25 minutes until mushrooms are cooked all the way through and the BBQ sauce is beginning to caramelize.

3. Allow to cool a bit, and then begin to shred them apart with 2 forks. You want nice jagged pieces, so get messy with them! Add more BBQ sauce if you want them on the saucier side.

4. Toast your buns in the oven under the broiler. Add a scoop of coleslaw, top with the pulled mushrooms, and finish with some pickles!

# Mains

This, to me, is the best part. The chef d'oeuvre. My magnum opus. I relish cooking and serving a main dish that I've been pouring my soul into all day. The chopping, stirring, braising, continually tasting, and re-adjusting, that's the kinda stuff that makes my little heart go pitter-patter. Well, that and the subsequent staring at any guest taking their first bite. TELL ME HOW GOOD IT IS!

"MY DOCTOR TOLD ME I HAD TO STOP THROWING INTIMATE DINNERS FOR FOUR UNLESS THERE ARE THREE OTHER PEOPLE."

—ORSON WELLES

# ALL DRESSED CHIPS CHOPS

*Serves 4*

It's a wacko idea, but it works! It's the perfectly Canadian patriotic dish. Canada has a lot to offer. (See: great bands, comedians, hockey players, the birthplace of basketball, and freaking awesome snacks, specifically chips.) So, while a majority of the world thinks of Canadian food as poutine (hopefully, you've already made my poutine recipe from the Snacks and Such chapter) and ketchup chips, y'all have been sleeping on All Dressed Chips, AND they're way more readily available in the US now. Anyways, here's how you make this masterpiece, which I think could totally pass as a Canadian Thanksgiving staple.

| | |
|---|---|
| 4 bone-in pork chops | 1 tsp. pepper |
| 1 family-size bag of Ruffles All Dressed Chips | 3 eggs |
| | 1-gallon Ziploc bag |
| 1 cup flour | wire cooling rack |
| 1 tsp. salt | |

1. Set oven to 425 degrees.

2. First order of business is crushing up the chips. God, I love chips. Toss them all in the Ziploc bag and start smashing. It helps to let a little of the air out of the bag so it doesn't pop while you're turning your chips to dust. I use my weighted rolling pin, but you can use whatever—hands, back of a pan, dealer's choice. You want all the chips ground down to about the same consistency.

3. Set up your dredging station. One bowl with the flour, salt, and pepper, stirred to combine. In the other bowl, whisk the three eggs like you're making scrambled eggs.

4. Pat the pork chops dry with a paper towel. Give them a little pinch of salt and pepper.

5. Toss them, one by one, into the flour mixture. Shake off excess flour, fully coat the chops in the egg dredge, and then throw 'em into the Ziploc bag and fully coat with the all-dressed-chips crumbs. Get in there. Get messy. You want them fully coated!

6. Place your cooling rack on your baking sheet so the heat can access all sides of the chops and you don't end up with a soggy side.

7. Now bake these sweet fatties for about 25 minutes. Keep an eye on them around the 20-minute mark. You can use a meat thermometer to check that the internal temp of 145 is reached.

8. LET THEM REST! This is crucial! Pork can get so dry, so letting them rest to let the juices settle is gonna make them juuuuuuicy!

9. Eat up! Don't look back. Welcome to the new Canadian National Dish.

# BACON AND TOMATO CLAMS

*Serves 2*

It's easy to feel like you're in way over your head when cooking shellfish in your own home, or that you could quite possibly food poison your loved ones and guests. But these little gems actually tell you when they're ready and when they're not. Within a few minutes of being added to some simmering savory wine-y broth, they open up to be presented to the world in their little shell platter like the sweet little baby clams in the Walrus and the Carpenter scene in *Alice in Wonderland*. Maybe those were oysters. Whatever. That scene has always haunted me. But if the clams aren't ready to eat, a.k.a. gone bad, they just won't open. Toss 'em out. Now, we all know that bacon goes with literally everything. Especially tomatoes. Adding lettuce to this dish makes literally zero sense, so it's not full-on BLT. But you get where I was going with this. If I'm just dipping buttered bread in clam broth and calling it dinner, I'm A-OK with that.

2 lbs. Manila clams

½ lb. bacon, cut into chunks

1 med. onion, chopped

1 tbsp. salted butter

4 vine tomatoes, chopped

3 cloves garlic, chopped

½ bottle of dry white wine

salt and pepper to season

parsley for garnish

1 French baguette

flakey salt. Maldon. I love this stuff so much!

1. Soak your clams in a bowl of cold water for about 20 minutes to get the sand and grit out. Then scrub each one down and really get into the little hinge part.

2. Cook your bacon until crispy and then remove from the pan. Let it sit on a plate covered with a paper towel to soak up the extra grease.

3. In that same pan, add the onion and the butter. Cook onions until tender, not browned, 3–4 min.

4. Add in the chopped tomato and let it reduce down a bit—4–5 minutes.

5. Add the garlic and stir to start to cook and release its delicious aroma. Adding it closer to the end makes the garlic flavor stand out more.

6. Add the ½ bottle of white wine. And, obviously, if you haven't already, pour yourself a glass, girl. You deserve it.

7. Toss in your sweet clams. Cover and let sit for a few minutes. Check back in on them after about 4–5 min and see how they're looking. Wait for them all to open up. If they haven't all opened within about 10 minutes, toss the ones that didn't make the team. Sayonara.

8. Divide among bowls and toss on some chopped parsley.

9. Slice up that crusty bread, butter it up. Finish with a little sprinkle of the flakey salt (it'll change lives).

10. Open more wine. Re-fill glass. And then go for it.

# BEEFY BEEF STEW

*Serves 6–8*

This bad boy is always a showstopper. I BLEEPING love stew. Especially one that's been kicking it in the oven low and slow in a broth that consists of an entire bottle of red wine. The flavors meld together and the beef just falls apart. Usually by the time it's done in the oven, I'm several glasses of wine in and ready for some decadence to be sopped up in some buttery crusty bread!

| | |
|---|---|
| 4 lbs. stewing beef, cut into 2-inch chunks | ½ tsp. pepper |
| 2 tbsp. olive oil | 1 tbsp. tomato paste |
| 3 turnips, peeled and cut into thick chunks | 2 bay leaves |
| 2 parsnips, peeled and cut into 1-inch chunks | sprigs of thyme |
| | 1 bottle of red wine |
| 2 carrots, peeled and cut into large chunks | 2 tbsp. flour |
| 1 large onion, cut into larger chunks | 1 cup water |
| 6 garlic cloves, minced | 1 cup beef broth |
| ½ tsp. salt | |

1. Generously salt and pepper the stewing beef in a large bowl, toss to coat. Do this the night before if you're smart and have planned ahead. I generally decide what I want for dinner at like 3 in the afternoon and have to skip that part.

2. In a Dutch oven, heat the olive oil. Then in batches, start to brown all sides of the beef, about 2 min per side. Remove the beef from the pot.

3. Add in the onion and garlic and cook until they start to soften.

4.  Then add in the rest of the veggies. Cook until all of the veggies start to soften. About 5–8 minutes. Your house should be smelling amazing right about now.

5.  Add in the tablespoon of tomato paste and coat the veggies. You'll notice the tomato paste starts to darken in color. This means you're on the right track.

6.  Add in the bay leaves and thyme, simmer until you can catch the smell of them doing their aromatic magic. Sprinkle in the 2 tbsp. of flour and coat the veggies. It's going to feel thick and you might panic and think you're gonna burn it. Don't worry, you're good, because here comes the booze. Pour yourself a glass first; ¾ of the bottle is perfect for the stew.

7.  Cook until the smell of alcohol has been cooked out of the wine, a few minutes. I'm obsessed with the smell of wine cooking down.

8.  Once everything returns to a simmer, add the beef back into the pot, juices and everything delicious that's collected on the plate. Pile all dat meat in.

9.  Then add the cup of water and cup of beef broth. Bring it all back to a slow simmer.

10. Throw it in the oven at 300 degrees for an hour. Remove from the oven. Be careful because it's both heavy and hot AF! Give it a solid stir and then place it back in the oven for another 45 min. Now your beef is fall-apart heaven.

11. Serve with crusty bread.

# CAST-IRON POT PIE

*Serves 4–6*

I go in hard on some pot pie. Have you ever stumbled home from the bar (or your couch) and opened your fridge up to the mighty glory that is a day-old chicken pot pie? It's really what carby-buttery-saucy dreams are made of. This one is special because we forego the bottom crust, which just ends up soggy and sad at the end anyways. Cook the whole thing in the cast-iron skillet and call it a damn day. This is a step away from the traditional chicken pot pie. Instead of the peas and carrots and whatever other frozen veggies you might have tucked away in the Upside Down of your fridge, this baby was created during the early days of fall while I was missing foliage and the only substitute was squash, sage, and all the lovely tastes of autumn. Everyone will love it. This is a crowd pleaser if you have a house full of hungry maniacs, or if you like to eat alone on the couch in solitude like me. Emotional eating is a hell of a good time. I don't care what anyone has to say about it. This is the ultimate comfort meal.

2 tbsp. olive oil

8 oz. mushrooms (I do baby bellas but this can be dealer's choice), sliced

2 chicken breasts, cut into even chunks

1 small onion, diced

½ butternut squash, cubed

3 cloves of garlic, minced

2 tbsp. fresh sage, chopped

4 sprigs thyme, chopped

2 cups chicken stock

½ cup whole milk

slurry (reserved ½ cup of chicken stock whisked together with 2 tbsp. flour)

salt and pepper to taste

frozen pie crust—keep it in the fridge until you're ready to use it

: 2 eggs

: 3 tbsp. water

A'ight—so let's shoot this straight, shall we? Have you ever tried to cut a squash? It's like some Navy Seal-level stuff and I'm always terrified of chopping off my entire hand. To cut your squash safely, ask someone else to do it, someone whose hands you care less about. OR, stab your squash a few times with a fork or knife and throw her in the microwave for 5 minutes to soften. Rotate and add another 5 if your squash needs it. Then proceed to slicing and dicing. Squash hacks!

## IN THE MEANTIME!

1. Preheat your oven to 400 degrees.

2. Over medium-high heat in your 12″ cast-iron skillet, heat the olive oil and begin to cook the onions until they become translucent. Then add in your 'shrooms to get these suckers to sweat out all of their lovely juices. Toss in your cut-up chicken breast and begin to cook through. Once the chicken is opaque and no more pink is visible, add the garlic. Toss in the thyme and sage and heat through until aromatic. Now would be a great time to add in your cubed squash. You want to keep the squash in chunks so it doesn't get all grainy and pulpy as it cooks.

3. Add in 1½ cups of chicken stock. (Save the other ½ cup of stock to make your slurry.) Bring to a simmer, then add in your ½ cup of milk. Bring it back to a simmer, and let it reduce a bit. About 10 minutes.

4. Make your slurry! Combine your ½ cup of stock with 2 tablespoons of flour. Whisk it together until there are no chunks. Slowly add the slurry to the skillet. Your mixture will start to thicken almost immediately. Salt and pepper to taste. Don't be shy. What's life without salt? Literally, we wouldn't exist. Salt away my friends. About 1 tsp. is a good starting point.

5. Remove from the heat and get that pie crust out of the fridge. (My mom is probably so annoyed I used a store-bought crust for this. TOO BAD, CAROLE!) Place your pie crust on top of the delicious chicken-y skillet and pinch the sides to seal the crust to the skillet. You can get fancy and do a cool-ass design or just pinch and seal, so long as it's sealed.

6. EGG WASH—whisk together the eggs and water and brush your egg wash onto the crust to ensure optimal golden delight.

7. TOSS THIS BAD BOY INTO THE OVEN. Use 2 hands, this dude is heavy. Bake for 40–45 minutes until the crust is golden brown. Let sit for 10 minutes before serving.

**SEMI PRO TIP**: You can prepare this in advance, store in the fridge, and pop it in the oven when it's closer to serving time! I love having all of the heavy lifting done before my guests arrive. That way dinner is ¾ of the way done and you've already had time to clean up and restore any chaos that may have broken out in the kitchen!

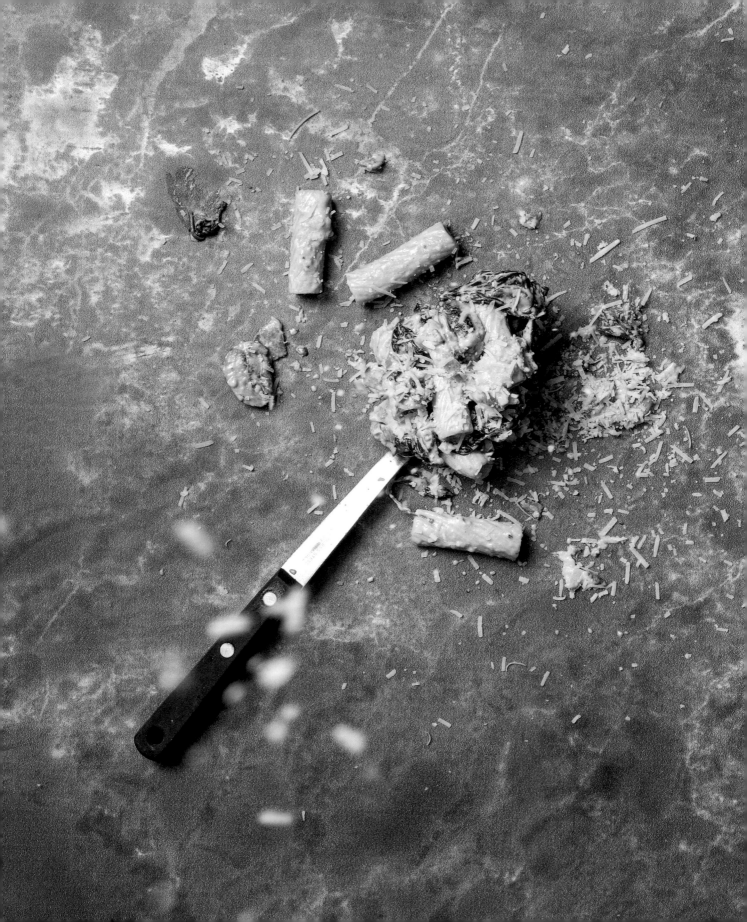

# CREAMY BACON SHROOM PASTA

*Serves 6*

I am obsessed with basically every pasta. I've never met a pasta I didn't like, but when I commit to a bowl of carbs, I want it to be creamy and garlicky and worth every single bite! This baby was born one evening when I was clearing out what was left in the fridge: mushrooms, bacon, parmesan, some baby spinach—because I thought I was going make a salad lolllll—and some cream. This was a dish even my husband loved, and he's not a big pasta guy. I know, it's one of his biggest shortcomings.

| | |
|---|---|
| 16 oz. bacon, cut into 2-inch chunks | ½ tsp. pepper |
| 8 oz. baby bella mushrooms, sliced | ½ tsp. salt |
| 2 cups spinach | ½ cup of pasta water |
| 2 garlic cloves, minced | 16 oz. pasta, I used rigatoni—but you do you, boo! |
| 2 cups of cream | |
| 1 cup grated parmesan | |

1. Bring a pot of water to a boil and cook pasta to al dente.

2. In a pan, crisp your bacon over medium heat, remove from pan with a slotted spoon to a paper-towel-lined plate to drain excess grease. Pour out the bacon grease but leave about 2 tablespoons of grease in the pan to cook the mushrooms.

3. Add the mushrooms to the pan; once they start to brown and release their liquid, add your garlic, salt, and pepper.

4.  Add in the cream and bring to a simmer. Stir in the parmesan and simmer for a few minutes until the sauce begins to thicken. Add the spinach and allow it to wilt, it'll only take a few minutes. Add the bacon back into the pasta sauce.

5.  Once your pasta is cooked and drained (and you reserved that ½ cup of the pasta water) add the noodles to the sauce, along with the ½ cup of pasta water, and toss to completely coat!

6.  Add more parmesan on top when serving, because...obviously!

7.  ENJOY!

# SPINACH AND ARTICHOKE STUFFED SHELLS

*Serves 6*

Ricotta may just be one of my favorite things. I could eat it out of the container and feel zero remorse. My intestines, however, may beg to differ. When you add in garlicky spinach, artichoke hearts, and MORE CHEESE; fill those pasta shells; add some tomato sauce and still MORE CHEESE; and then bake it, it's Drool City, USA. It should be noted that these are also very good the next day cold out of the fridge.

16 oz. large pasta shells

3 cups marinara sauce

16 oz. whole milk ricotta

1 cup shredded mozzarella

1 cup parmesan, plus more to top

4 cups spinach

2 garlic cloves, minced

1 14 oz. can artichoke hearts, drained

2 tbsp. olive oil

1 tsp. salt

1 tsp. pepper

2 eggs

½ cup fresh basil, chopped

1. Preheat your oven to 375 degrees.

2. Bring a large pot of salted water to a boil and cook your shells about a minute or two shorter than the box directions. Around 6–7 minutes for the brand I used. We want al dente here, because they will continue to cook once you pop them in the oven. Once the pasta is ready, drain it and allow to cool for when it's stuffing time.

3. Meanwhile, heat the oil in a large pan and add the garlic. Sauté over medium heat until that beautiful garlicky smell takes over your face. Add the spinach and cook until it's wilted down, only a few minutes.

4. In a food processer, add the ricotta, spinach, artichokes, mozzarella, salt, pepper, and eggs. Pulse the mixture a few times to blend together. You don't want to puree this mixture, just incorporate it all together and break up the artichoke hearts.

5. In a greased 9x12 baking dish, evenly pour 1 cup of the marinara sauce. Now it's time to stuff these shells, baby! I used a tablespoon to stuff the ricotta mixture into the shells. If you wanna get all super fancy and use a piping bag, be my guest! Pack as many of the stuffed shells into the dish as you can, cover in the remaining marinara sauce, and top with the fresh basil and parmesan.

6. Pop the shells in the oven for about 25–30 minutes until bubbling, when the cheese is getting all golden and delicious.

7. Allow to sit for about 10 minutes before serving.

# SEAFOOD SQUID INK PASTA

*Serves 4*

This dish should actually be called Panty Dropper Pasta. There's something so fancy-pants about eating an ink-black pasta. The briney-ness of the cuttlefish ink gives this pasta a swift kick in the ass and asserts itself as a "you wanna hit it tonight?" kinda sexiness. Is pasta sexy? This one wouldn't last 10 minutes on Tinder. Or Grinder. Love is love, and this pasta can get it. The first time I made this was for Valentine's Day, and I figured if I went above and beyond in the kitchen, my husband would do the same in the sack. Let's just say…get that cuttlefish Amazon Primed to your house. Yes, you can buy cuttlefish ink on Amazon. What a time to be alive. Enjoy, lovers!

| | |
|---|---|
| 1 tbsp. cuttlefish or squid ink | 4 eggs |
| 3 cups of flour ('00' flour or semolina flour if you have it. If not, all-purpose works too!) | 2 tbsp. water |
| | 2 tbsp. olive oil |
| | ½ tsp. salt |

## TO MAKE THE PASTA!

Making your own pasta makes you feel very freaking cool. It's truly pretty easy, and it provides a HUGE payoff when you drop your little nests of midnight black pasta into your pot of salted boiling water.

1. To help make sure that your pasta is evenly black, mix your cuttlefish ink with the 4 eggs and give it a good whisk.

2. In your stand mixer (I totally recommend using one; I use the KitchenAid, and the pasta attachments are *chef's kiss*) add your flour and salt, then make a tiny well in the middle of the flour to add in your ink/egg mixture, followed by the olive oil and water. With your paddle attachment, mix on low for a minute or two until the dough JUST starts to come together. Then go ahead and switch the paddle attachment to the dough-hook attachment. Let it mix on low/med for about 3–5 minutes. You want your dough to have some bounce to it. If your dough is too wet, add a tablespoon of flour. If it's looking a bit too crumbly, add water by the tablespoon until you have a soft, bouncy, black ball of dough!

3. Cut your dough in half and roll each half into a ball and cover with Saran Wrap. Let it chill in the fridge for at least an hour.

4. Before you start the magic that is actually turning this ball of heaven into real-life pasta, remove it from the fridge and let it come to room temp so its elasticity can come back and allow it to feed through the pasta roller with ease! About 30 minutes.

5. With the first of the 2 halves of dough, go ahead and cut into quarters and roll each section out on a floured surface to about ½ an inch of thickness.

6. Attach your pasta roller to your stand mixer and start out with the thickest setting so that the dough doesn't get jammed in the roller. Keep the speed low.

7. Start feeding your pasta through at the top of the pasta roller. Repeat this process and start to adjust the thickness of the pasta roller so your sheet of pasta gets progressively thinner and thinner, to your liking. Usually around level 6 or 7 is good.

8. As you're working your pasta through the roller, keep in mind that flour will be your pal and help keep things moving smoothly. So, just as you would add flour to the surface you're working on when baking, do the same here!

9. Repeat this process, with all of the dough through the roller before attaching the pasta cutter.

10. Once you're happy with the thickness of your pasta, remove the pasta roller and attach the pasta cutter. This is chef's choice. If you want linguine or spaghetti, then go for it. Feed it through the cutter. This is one of the most satisfying moments of all time. Enjoy the sweet satisfaction.

11. I like to spin my pasta into a little nest and lay it out on a parchment-paper-lined baking sheet, but if you have a pasta-drying tree, do your thang!

12. And now, my sweet, sweet handsome friends, it's time to start cooking! Bring a large pot of salted water to a boil and drop in your pasta. Cook to al dente, about 4 minutes. Drain your pasta but reserve a ½ cup of the pasta water.

## TO MAKE THE SAUUUUUCE

| | |
|---|---|
| 1 shallot, diced | 1 lb. shrimp, uncooked, peeled— leaving the tails on |
| 3 cloves of garlic | |
| 1 28 oz. can whole tomatoes | ½–¾ cup dry white wine |
| 2 tbsp. olive oil | ½ cup pasta water |
| 2 tbsp. unsalted butter | pinch red pepper flakes |
| 2 lbs. clams—I used Manila | fresh parmesan |
| | parsley |

1. Add oil and butter to large pan or Dutch oven. Over medium heat, add in diced shallot and garlic. Cook until the shallot becomes translucent. Add in the red pepper flakes and cook another 30 seconds. Add in the whole tomatoes, but not their sauce. Crush them with your hands for a rustic chunky vibe. We want to keep this mostly a white wine sauce, but I can never help myself and always want to add tomatoes. Start to cook the tomatoes down. About 3–4 minutes. Then add the white wine. Let that simmer until the smell of alcohol is cooked out of the sauce. (Sad, I know. It's okay, pour yourself a goblet now, too.) Add in your clams. Cover and let them cook. About 6–7 minutes. They let you know when you're done when they all start to open up. Any ones that don't open up in about 10 minutes, throw them out. They're not okay to eat.

2. Now it's time to remove the clams. Set them to the side for a hot minute. Add in your shrimp to cook through, until they're pink and opaque, about 4–5 minutes. Meanwhile, leave about ¼ of your clams in their shell, ya know, for the aesthetic. Take the rest, remove clams from the shells, and roughly chop those little babies up. Add them back into the sauce. Now add in your ½ cup of reserved pasta water, and your fresh squid-y pasta. Toss it in the sauce for a minute or two and let the noodles absorb some of your garlicy, clammy, wine-y sauce.

3. Divide evenly amongst bowls! Top with fresh grated parmesan and a sprinkle of parsley.

# SPICY CINCINNATI CHILI

*Serves 6–8*

Here's the thing: if you've never had Cincinnati chili, go ahead and throw all of your ideas about chili out the door. When you're married to a man from The 'Nati, you must accept this into your life. In Cincinnati, there's the age-old debate about which you prefer—Skyline or Gold Star Chili. Personally, I'm Skyline all day, baby!! So, I wanted to try and make my own to curb those Midwest cravings. I've added a little more kick to it. This chili is far more liquidy than what you're used to. No big meat chunks. No beans. And there's cinnamon and chocolate in it. It's an acquired taste, but trust me, it's freaking delicious. Also, there are all the different ways it can be served. More on that later.

The key here is to literally just combine all the ingredients in a large heavy pot, simmer and stir until desired consistency. Easy peasy. It takes about 2–2½ hours. WORTH IT! While it simmers, you sip.

6 cups water

2 lbs. ground beef (I've made this with bison!)

1 medium yellow onion, diced

4 garlic cloves, minced

1 tbsp. tomato paste

1 cup tomato sauce

3 tbsp. chili powder

1½ tsp. cumin

1 tsp. cinnamon

1 tsp. allspice

½ tsp. ground cloves

½ tsp. cayenne

1 tsp. salt

2 tbsp. Worcestershire sauce

1 tbsp. white vinegar

1 oz. unsweetened chocolate (if it comes in a bar with breakable cubes, just break the cubes into their ¼ oz. individual cubes—4 of them—and toss them in the mixture, no need to grate it up. It'll melt.)

Bring the water to a boil, add in your ground beef, and begin to break up the meat; this is what the texture of the Cinci chili is all about. The meat gets thin and broken up. Add all of the other ingredients. No need to soften the onion or garlic, just drop everything in, bring it back to a boil. Reduce the heat to medium-low and simmer for about 2 hours with a lid half on. You don't want the lid on all the way or else the steam won't release, the liquid won't reduce, and it'll be simmering for days. Keep an eye on your chili and stir occasionally. Once everything is beautifully combined and a quarter of the liquid has reduced, you should be in pretty good business. Now you're ready to decide which way you want to enjoy this pot of spicy chili goodness.

## THE WAYS by THE KING OF CINCINNATI, JON MOXLEY

This chili is deployed onto the battlefield chiefly by 2 methods: hot dogs and spaghetti. Cheese Coneys are hot dogs topped with chili and shredded cheddar cheese. The addition of mustard and onion is optional. In my opinion, there are 3 keys to an authentic Cincinnati cheese Coney: 1. Dog must be boiled 2. Bun must be steamed. 3. Cheese must be fluffy. At Skyline, all these elements blend together in a seamless Coney experience. The next major way to serve Cincinnati style chili is over spaghetti utilizing the "way" system:

2-way—Spaghetti topped with chili

3-way (most popular)—Spaghetti, chili, and cheese

4-way onion—Spaghetti, chili, cheese, and diced yellow onion

4-way bean—spaghetti, chili, cheese, and kidney beans

5-way—ALL OF IT! Spaghetti, chili, cheese, onions, and beans

Chili can also simply be served in a bowl by itself or topped with cheese. Other traditional ancillary tools in the Cincinnati-style chili game include oyster crackers and tabasco sauce.

SEMI PRO TIP: I suggest YouTube-ing the Skyline theme song while preparing this Ohio delicacy.

For optimal cheese fluffiness—grate your cheddar cheese using the longest side of the block of cheese against the smallest grate on your cheese grater. It creates longer, lighter cheese clouds!

To steam the hotdog bun: soak a few pieces of paper towel in water. Squeeze out as much water as possible and wrap it around your hotdog bun. Microwave 15–30 seconds for optimal steaminess!

# CINCI CHILI DIP

*Serves 6–8*

I'm assuming you have spicy Cincinnati chili leftovers. You've had some on a coney, had the oyster crackers, the spaghetti, but what now? MAKE A DIP! A LAYERED DIP! Few things are such surefire smash hits as layered dips. They're at every WrestleMania and Super Bowl party. They're easy to prep in advance, and everyone loves to scoop up the perfect bite on a chip.

2 cups of Cincinnati chili

2 cups sour cream

1 cup tomatoes, diced

1 cup onion, diced

2 cups shredded cheddar cheese

1½ cups shredded lettuce

1 bag of tortilla chips

In a pie dish or casserole dish, spoon in the sour cream and evenly distribute. Add the chili and smooth out the edges. Sprinkle on the tomatoes and onion. Add the nice layer of shredded cheese and finish off with a layer of fresh shredded lettuce. Keep in the fridge until ready to serve. Serve cold with tortilla chips.

# CRAB-STUFFED TOMATOES

*Serves 6–8*

I really enjoy stuffing things with other things. Like any other red-blooded woman, I can't resist the rich, cheesy, burn-the-roof-of-your-mouth-every-damn-time crab and artichoke dip. Being the culinary maverick that I am, I figured that tomatoes should be filled to the brim with it and then served as its own, well-rounded dish. Protein, dairy, and veggies. Basically, this is your keto dream meal. Are people still doing keto? For the love of breadcrumbs, please say no.

| | |
|---|---|
| 12 medium tomatoes | 1 cup parmesan (divided into ½ cups) |
| 1 lb. lump crab meat | 1 tsp. salt |
| 8 oz. cream cheese | ½ tsp. pepper |
| 1 can (14 oz.) artichoke hearts, drained and finely diced | 1 tbsp. lemon juice |
| 2 garlic cloves, minced | 1 tbsp. butter, melted |
| 1 cup shredded mozzarella | ½ cup breadcrumbs |

1. Preheat your oven to 375 degrees.

2. Rinse the tomatoes and cut a thin layer off the top. Run a sharp knife along the inside of the tomato to separate the flesh and seeds from the skin. Scoop out the insides with a spoon. Don't go too thin because you still need the tomato to be sturdy when you stuff and bake them. Cut a thin layer off the bottom of the tomatoes as well so that they will stand upright on the baking sheet. Sprinkle the insides of the tomatoes with some salt, as you want to drain out as much of the water as you can. On a wire rack, place the tomatoes upside down to allow the water to drain. Allow them to sit about 10 minutes.

3. Meanwhile, in Crab Town, let's get the real party started. In a large mixing bowl, combine the crab, artichokes, cream cheese (pop it in the microwave for about 30 seconds if it's not soft enough), mozzarella, ½ cup of the parmesan, garlic, salt, pepper, and lemon juice. Mix together until fully combined.

4. Mix together the breadcrumbs, butter, and remaining ½ cup of parmesan for the topping.

5. Stuff the tomatoes with the crab mixture and sprinkle the tops with about 1 tbsp. of the breadcrumbs each. Place the tomatoes on a lined baking sheet and bake them in the oven for about 30 minutes until bubbling and the breadcrumbs turn golden brown.

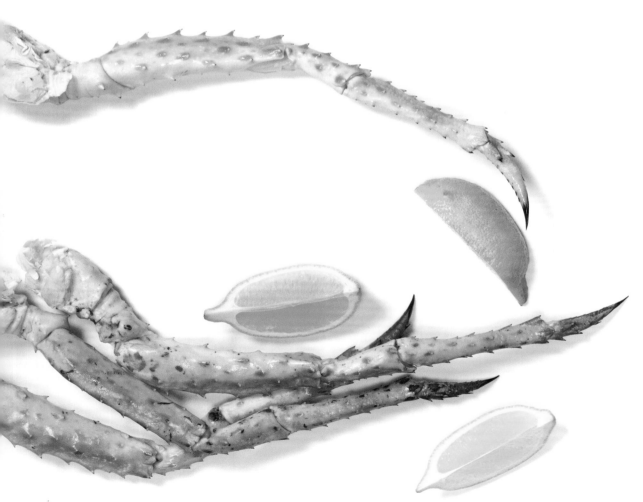

# ONE-PAN SHRIMP FAJITAS

*Serves 4–6*

This baby right here is a standard Paquette/Good/Moxley household go-to. Set up a DIY station so everyone can prepare theirs exactly how they like. This is a flavor-packed meal that is all said and done in about 30 minutes, with only one baking sheet to clean up after! More time for margaritas and watercooler chit-chat!

## FAJITA SEASONING

- 1 tbsp. chili powder
- 1 tsp. garlic powder
- ½ tsp. onion powder
- ¼ tsp. chili flakes
- ¼ tsp. oregano
- ½ tsp. smoked paprika
- 2 tsp. cumin

In a small bowl, mix together the spices for the fajita seasoning.

## SHRIMP N VEGGIES

- 1 lb. raw shrimp
- 1 cup green pepper, julienned
- 1 cup red peppers, julienned
- 1 cup red onion, julienned
- 1 cup baby mushrooms, diced
- ¼ cup olive oil

1.  Preheat oven to 425 degrees.

2.  In a larger bowl, after removing the shells and tails, add the raw shrimp. (Thaw in cool water if you're using frozen shrimp.) Add the peppers and mushrooms. You can add whatever veggies you like here;, these are just my go-to. Toss to coat in the olive oil and fajita seasoning.

3.  Transfer the shrimp and veggies to a lined baking sheet. Evenly distribute so that there's not too much overlapping. Toss in the oven for about 25 minutes.

## EXTRAS

- shredded lettuce
- shredded cheddar
- sour cream
- salsa
- cilantro
- flour tortillas

Serve on tortillas with whatever toppings you're into. My go-to for fajitas is a heap of sour cream, salsa, lettuce, cheddar, and cilantro!

# PASTA PRIMAVERA

*Serves 6–8*

What a beautiful spring-y delight. There are so many veggies that you won't feel bad about indulging in the pasta and extremely light lemony cream sauce…or storing it in your fridge and secretly spooning mouthfuls into your face in the middle of the night. This recipe can totally be adapted into your own version, because it's an easy way to incorporate any leftover veggies that might be on their last days in the fridge. Use whatever you have! And if you're itching to add some protein, chicken or shrimp, toss 'em in!

16 oz. rigatoni (Or any spiral/textured pasta)

½ cup pasta water reserved

½ cup green pepper, diced

½ cup red pepper, diced

½ cup orange pepper, diced

¾ cup cherry or grape tomatoes, halved

1 cup broccoli spears, loosely chopped

1 cup baby bella mushrooms, diced

1 cup yellow squash, diced

½ cup asparagus, diced

½ cup onion, diced

½ cup frozen peas

2 cups spinach

1 cup heavy cream

4 tbsp. butter

juice of one lemon, about 2 tablespoons

1 tsp. salt

½ tsp. pepper

½ tsp. red pepper flakes

2 garlic cloves, minced

¾ cup parmesan

fresh basil to top

1. Bring a large pot of salted water to a boil and cook your rigatoni according to the directions on the box. Al dente, baby. Remember to reserve ½ cup of the pasta water.

2. Meanwhile, in a large pan, heat 2 tbsp. of oil and add the peppers, mushrooms, and onions and begin to soften. You want to just start the cooking process. You're not looking to brown the vegetables. Then add the tomatoes, asparagus, yellow squash, and broccoli. Heat through. Remove from heat, salt and pepper to season, and then add your frozen peas and spinach. They'll cook in the residual heat.

3. Time for the saucy sauce. In a medium pan, melt the butter, add the garlic, and cook until fragrant. Add the heavy cream and bring to a simmer. Toss in your parmesan and stir until it's all melted and incorporated. Add the lemon juice and ¼ cup of the pasta water.

4. In a large bowl, or if your pot is big enough, combine the pasta, vegetables, and lemon cream sauce. Toss to fully coat with the sauce, then add the remaining ¼ cup of pasta water if your sauce needs to be thinned out. Top with more parmesan and fresh basil to serve.

# PEANUT BUTTER AND JELLY CHICKEN

*Serves 4–6*

Hear. Me. Out. Does this sound like I ate a special brownie and just invented some random meal? Yes, it sounds exactly like that; however, I did not. I only come up with good ideas when I'm several bottles of wine deep. But it doesn't take a rocket scientist to know that PB&J are delicious on any and everything. Without further ado, I'd like to give a shout out to my culinary brilliance for bringing this dish together, ahhhhthankyouverymuch! PB&J is the first flavor tag team that a majority of us ever fell in love with. There's a comfort and familiarity with these salty/sweet worlds uniting. Then add some chiiiiiiicken and enjoy!

2- 2 ½ lbs. boneless skinless chicken thighs

1 cup unsweetened coconut milk

1 tbsp. grated ginger

2 garlic cloves, minced

1 tbsp. fish sauce

1 tbsp. lime juice

1 tbsp. sugar

1 tbsp. chili garlic paste

wood or metal skewers

½ cup smooth peanut butter

¼ cup unsweetened coconut milk

2 tbsp. low-sodium soy sauce

3 tbsp. water

1 tbsp. apple cider vinegar

1 tbsp. brown sugar

1 pint raspberries

1 pint blackberries

¾ cup sugar

½ cup water

1 tbsp. lemon juice

½ cup crushed peanuts

fresh cilantro

1. First things first, we gotta marinate that chicken. Cut the chicken thighs up into about 2-in strips. In a large mixing bowl, add the coconut milk, ginger, garlic, fish sauce, lime juice, sugar, and chili garlic paste. Mix it together well and add the chicken. Toss to fully coat, cover, and allow to marinate in the fridge for at least 30 minutes; 1–2 hours is best, though!

2. Meanwhile, make the berry sauce. In a medium saucepan add in the berries, sugar, water, and lemon juice, and bring to a low simmer. Using the back of a fork or spoon, break up the berries as much as you can. Some chunks are totally okay. Who doesn't love the good pop of a full berry? Allow to simmer over low heat for about 15–20 minutes until the sauce has reduced and nicely coats the back of a spoon. Allow to cool at room temperature until ready to serve.

3. The insane peanut butter sauce! I could honestly eat this stuff off of anything. ANYTHING! Combine the peanut butter, coconut milk, soy sauce, fish sauce, water, apple cider vinegar, and brown sugar. Simmer for about 10 minutes. Remove from heat. Reserve about 1 cup of the sauce for drizzling/dipping. The rest will go on the chicken as you grill it.

4. Heat your grill to medium. Add the chicken to the skewers. Evenly divide the meat between 6–8 skewers. Place them all on the grill and allow to cook for about 2–3 minutes. Flip them over. Start applying the peanut butter sauce to the cooked side of the chicken. Cook for another 2–3 minutes and flip again. Apply more peanut butter sauce. Cook for 2–3 more minutes; add more sauce. The peanut butter sauce will start to caramelize with the heat of the grill. Once the chicken is fully cooked through, remove from the grill and drizzle with ½ cup of the reserved peanut butter sauce. Add crushed peanuts and cilantro if you're using them. Serve with remaining peanut and berry sauces for dipping.

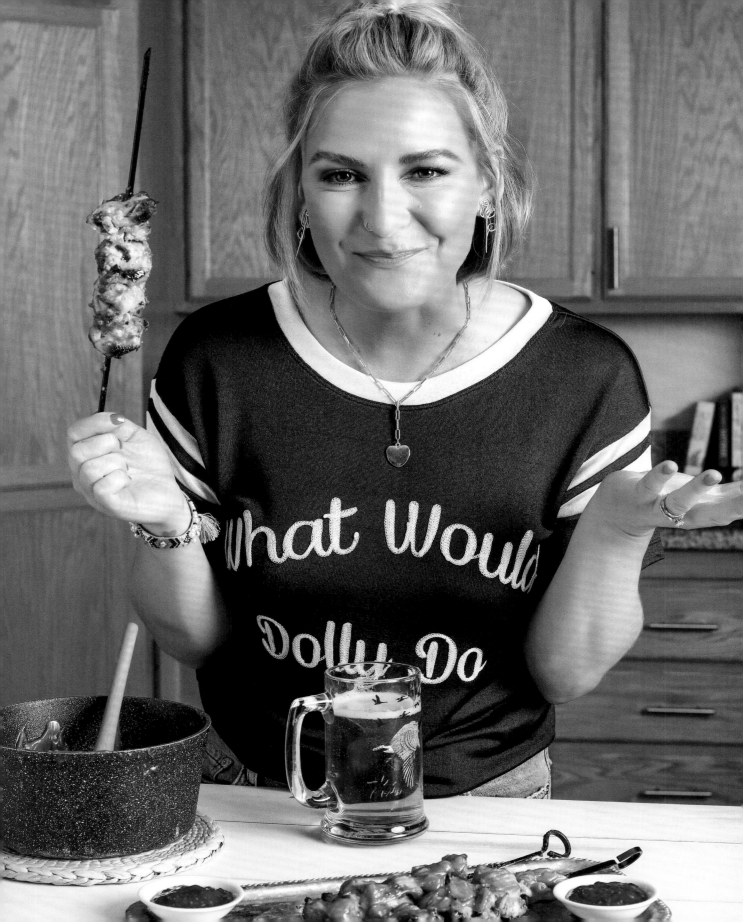

# SALMON GRAIN BOWL WITH LEMON TAHINI SAUCE

*Serves 4*

This is probably the meal I consume the most. It's healthy and packed with vitamins—all the good fats from the salmon and tahini, plus tons of veggies! This is a great way to clear out some vegetables from your fridge, as well. Hence, this is why I probably end up making it so often. Salmon has become one of my favorite proteins. More often than not, I pick up a filet when I swing by the grocery store. I prefer eating this meal at room temperature or cold, so I end up roasting the vegetables earlier in the day and get the farro or quinoa cooked earlier in the day, too. Then just top with some salmon, tahini sauce, and some fresh herbs! This is a meal you can feel good about and make your own. Use whatever vegetables are calling your name.

1½ lbs. salmon filets. I normally just buy 2 smaller fillets and divide them amongst the bowls

1 tsp. lemon pepper seasoning

¼ tsp. salt

1 cup farro or quinoa

2 cups water

1 cup broccoli, torn into smaller bite-sized pieces

1 cup zucchini or yellow squash, diced

1 cup sweet potato, diced

1 cup asparagus, cut into spears

¼ cup olive oil

½ tsp. salt

½ tsp. pepper

one bunch of cilantro

¼ cup tahini

¼ tsp. salt

½ tsp. pepper

zest of lemon

2–3 tbsp. fresh lemon juice

2 tbsp. water

1. Preheat your oven to 400 degrees.

2. On a lined baking sheet, combine all of your vegetables. You want enough for an even layer, and not so many that they are on top of each other. Drizzle with olive oil, salt, and pepper and mix well to completely coat all the vegetables. Bake about 20–25 minutes until fully roasted and beginning to crisp.

3. Cook your grain according to package directions—1 cup of grain to 2 cups of water.

4. Season the salmon filet with the salt and lemon pepper seasoning. In a large pan (preferably one with a lid), heat 2 tbsp. olive oil over medium heat. Once the oil is heated, add your salmon, skin side down. Place that lid on the pan. Allow to cook for about 5–6 minutes depending on the thickness of your filet. Flip the salmon over and continue to cook for another 5 minutes. Remove from heat and allow to continue to cook in the residual heat from the pan until flakey and opaque all the way through.

5. In a bowl, combine the tahini, lemon zest and juice, water, salt, and pepper. Whisk together until fully combined.

6. To serve: evenly distribute the grains amongst the bowls, top with roasted veggies, salmon, lemon tahini sauce, and a healthy dose of fresh herbs! Sprinkle with some flakey salt to add a little salty crunch!

**SEMI PRO TIP**: Tahini thickens as you start to mix it, so continue to add water a tablespoon at a time until desired consistency. I like mine a little on the thin side so I can drizzle it over the grain bowl.

Adding ¼ tsp. of toasted sesame oil to your grains really packs a punch. It's potent stuff, so don't use a heavy hand when tinkering with this flavor.

Other vegetables that are great to roast: tomatoes, squash, mushrooms, whole garlic cloves, onions, carrots, and turnip—whatever happens to be in season. Just try and cut each vegetable into roughly the same size so they roast at the same time.

# SHEPHERD'S PIE PIEROGIES

*Serves 4–6*

Pierogis get the shepherd's pie treatment! When I first started thinking about writing a cookbook, I kept mulling over what some of my favorite foods are and hoping that MAYBE, if I smashed some of them together, I'd strike gold and create some kind of delicious monster. I love a pierogi. We used to always have bags of frozen potato-and-cheddar pierogis in our freezer. Just pop them in some water and/or fry them and dip away to my heart's content in sour cream or a melted garlic butter concoction. Now, I would commit tiny petty crimes for a great shepherd's pie. Meat and potatoes baked into a casserole? Why not combine these heavenly creatures and see what happens? I was quite pleased with my findings.

## DOUGH

- 2 cups all-purpose flour
- ½ tsp. salt
- 3 tbsp. butter, room temperature
- 3 tbsp. water
- 1 egg
- ½ cup sour cream

## FILLING

- 2 tbsp. olive oil
- 1 cup onion, diced
- 2 garlic cloves, minced
- 1 lb. ground lamb or beef
- 2 tsp. parsley, chopped
- 1 tsp. rosemary, chopped
- ½ tsp. salt
- ½ tsp. pepper
- 1 tbsp. Worcestershire sauce
- 2 tbsp. tomato paste
- 2 tbsp. flour
- 1 cup beef broth
- 1 cup frozen peas

## MASHED POTATOES

See Herb Infused Mashed Potatoes on p. 81; cut recipe in half.

1. For the dough, combine the flour with the salt and add in butter and the wet ingredients and knead until a sticky ball has been formed. Cover with plastic wrap and leave in the fridge until ready to use. At least 30 minutes.

2. In a large pan, heat the olive oil over medium-high heat. Add the onion and cook until translucent. Add the ground lamb, begin to break up with the back of a spoon, and start to cook through. Once most of the meat is browned, drain out some of the fat and add in the garlic, parsley, and rosemary. Allow the herbs to become aromatic. Add the salt, pepper, Worcestershire sauce, and tomato paste. Cook the tomato paste until it starts to become more of a brown color. About 2 minutes. Add in ½ cup of the beef broth, reserving the other ½ cup for the slurry. In a small bowl or container whisk together the 2 tbsp. of flour and the ½ cup of reserved beef broth. When fully combined, slowly add to the meat mixture. The sauce will begin to thicken up. Allow to simmer over medium heat for about 5–8 minutes until the sauce has fully thickened up. Remove from heat and add the frozen peas. Combine meat mixture with about 2½ cups of the Herb Infused Mashed Potatoes.

3. Remove the dough from the fridge and begin to roll it out on a lightly floured surface. You want to roll the dough out to about ⅛ in. Using a cookie cutter, or even a mug, something around 3–4 inches in diameter, cut out the pierogi dumplings.

4. Now, time to stuff these babies! Have a bowl of water close by for sealing the pierogis. Place the dough in the palm of your hand. Using a tablespoon, place enough filling in the center of the dough so that you can still easily fold it and seal it. Using your finger, spread a small amount of water on one of the interior edges of the pierogi and pinch closed until sealed the entire way around.

5. In a pot of boiling, salted water, add a few pierogis at a time so you don't crowd the sweet little dumplings and have them stick together. You'll know when they're done once they float up to the surface. About 4–5 minutes. You can totally stop here. Orrrrrr you can have CRISPY PIEROGIS.

6. In a frying pan, add 2 tbsp. of butter and fry them about 2 minutes per side. GO TO SHEPHERDS PIE PIEROGI TOWN. BECOME THE MAYOR OF THAT TOWN!

# COCONUT CURRY RED SNAPPER

*Serves 4*

Remain calm! I assure you that cooking a whole fish is not beyond your skill set. It's ridiculously easy and feels suuuuuper-duper fancy when you serve it up to guests. Or maybe you're just treating your own damn self. Sometimes we gotta be fancy all by ourselves. The biggest thing I've learned from cooking a whole fish is asking the fishmonger at the local market or grocery store to scale and gut it. GAME CHANGER! My father-in-law once brought a whole fish to my house to try to teach me how to do this on my own…and let me tell you from my own experience: bring in the pros. They know what they're doing.

This recipe goes swimmingly—hahaakjhdajhdlakdha—I'll see myself out—with the Coconut Rice and Mango Salad.

| | |
|---|---|
| 3 lb. red snapper (any fresh white fish that's not overfished will do) | 2 tbsp. olive oil |
| 1 lemon, sliced | 1 cup yellow onion, diced |
| 1 bunch cilantro | 2 garlic cloves, minced |
| 2 green onions, white and light green ends. | 2 tbsp. fresh ginger, minced or Microplaned |
| 2–3 tbsp. olive oil | 1 tbsp. tomato paste |
| ½ tsp. salt | 1 cup diced tomatoes and their juices |
| ½ tsp. pepper | 2 tbsp. curry powder (I used a mild yellow curry) |
| | 1 can coconut milk |
| | 1 tbsp. fish sauce |
| | ½ tsp. salt |

1. Preheat oven to 450 degrees.

2. Score the fish along both sides in diagonal slices. Brush on olive oil. Sprinkle the skin and inside cavity with salt and pepper. Stuff the inside cavity of the fish with lemon slices, cilantro, and green onion. It will be coming out of the bottom a little bit but that's totally ok.

3. On a parchment-paper-lined baking sheet, place in the oven for about 20 minutes or until the meat is opaque and flakey.

4. In a medium-sized saucepan heat the olive oil over medium heat. Add the onions and cook until translucent. About 3–5 minutes. Add the garlic and ginger and stir until fragrant, about 2 minutes. Add the tomato paste and cook until it deepens in color to almost a brown shade, about one minute. Add the cup of diced tomatoes and coconut milk. Return to a simmer. Add the curry powder and fish sauce and simmer for another 8–10 minutes until the sauce has reduced a bit. Salt and pepper to taste.

5. Cover the fish in the curry sauce and extra cilantro and green onion.

6. Serve with Coconut Rice and Mango Salad.

# WHOLE CHICKEN WITH CRISPY POTATOES

*Serves 4*

Cooking a whole chicken makes me feel like a '50s housewife. I mean that in the absolute best way. I think I would have thrived in that era. Roll up your sleeves and make a beautiful crispy-skinned bird that's fresh out the oven when your significant other waltzes through the door. Carve up this handsome bird and then blow his/her mind with the crispy potatoes. All while wearing a fashion house dress and tossing 2–3 glasses of wine down the hatch. I WOULD HAVE THRIVED!

The key here is the potatoes. You pull the entire chicken/potato situation out of the oven and, while the chicken rests all of its sweet, sweet juices, you smash your potatoes and toss 'em back in the oven to crisp IN THE CHICKEN FAT! WHAT?! Ina has the engagement chicken, this should be called the pregnancy chicken, because girl…you're about to GET IT! (Or guy—either way, babies are being made.)

| | |
|---|---|
| 1 3-4 lb. chicken | 1 lb. baby potatoes—enough to surround the chicken in the cast iron skillet |
| 4 tbsp. softened butter | |
| 1 tbsp. salt | 2 tbsp. olive oil |
| ½ tsp. pepper | 1 tsp. salt |
| 1 whole garlic bulb, cut in half to expose the garlic | ½ tsp. pepper |
| 1 yellow onion, cut into wedges | |
| 1 bunch of thyme/rosemary. About 8 sprigs thyme, 3 rosemary sprigs | |

1. Preheat your oven to 425 degrees.

2. To prepare your chicken, remove any of the giblets that may be left inside and pluck any stray feathers that may have clung on.

3. Take 2 tablespoons of the butter and spread it between the chicken breast and the skin. To do this, just run your fingers along the layer of skin and gently pull it away from the chicken breast. Spread the butter as evenly as you can between the skin and the meat. Use the remaining 2 tbsp. of butter on the outside of the chicken. Spread it all over the surface of the chicken. Then layer the chicken, inside and out, with the salt and pepper. Stuff the entire bulb of garlic inside the chicken, along with half of the onion that's been cut into wedges (the other half will join the potatoes), and then, finally, add the thyme/rosemary combo. You're ready to tie up your bird. This is necessary for the chicken to cook evenly in the oven. If you're confused on how to do it—YouTube it. It's easier to watch someone do it than my dumb ass trying to type it out.

4. In your cast-iron skillet, add your cleaned baby potatoes, olive oil, and salt and pepper. Combine well to coat the potatoes. Move the potatoes to form a circle in the pan to create a nest for the chicken to hang out while it's roasting. Drop your chicken in that little potato nest. Put it in the oven for about 1½ hours. Check it around this time. The internal temperature should reach 165 degrees. Insert your thermometer between the thigh and the body for the temperature because the dark meat will take longer.

5. Remove your chicken from the skillet and allow to rest on your cutting board.

6. Turn up the heat in the oven to 475 degrees.

7. Use the bottom of a mug or something with a flat bottom to slightly smash your potatoes. Just enough to break them open but not to totally lose their shape. Spread them evenly around the cast-iron skillet and return to the oven for 10–12 minutes. They'll be nice and crispy on the outside and soft and buttery on the inside!

8. Carve up your bird, serve, and enjoy.

# FANCY AF BEEF TENDERLOIN

*Serves 6*

Yes. Yes. Mother eff yes. Of all the things I've ever made, this is one of my favorites! Every single year I struggle to decide what to make for Christmas dinner. Because you see, friends, in Canada, our Thanksgiving is in October, and our Christmas is on, well Christmas. Traditionally, my family would do turkey dinner for both holidays. But now, with my time spent in the great ol' US of A, I've realized that's a bit of a faux pas with Thanksgiving and Jesus's birthday being mere weeks apart. Do I make a fancy pasta? Do I do a ham? Do we order in Chinese? Well, let me tell you, literally all of those other ideas can piss up a rope. This tenderloin is heaven! It's cooked to a perfect medium pink, excellently crusted, and cuts like a hot knife through sweet Irish butter. This is one I will return to time and time again. It doesn't take ages to cook, and, no joke, I saw my vegetarian brother deeply reconsider his life choice, but sadly, he stuck to his guns. Here we go!

3 lbs. beef tenderloin

1 tbsp. salt

½ tbsp. pepper

½ tsp. crushed red pepper flakes

1 tbsp. fresh rosemary

4 cloves of garlic

2 tbsp. EVOO

1. Mash all of these ingredients into a paste of sorts. Rub it on your loin, wrap it up, and let it hang out in the fridge overnight, or at least a few hours. I'm a big fan of an overnight marinade, especially with this, to let the salt penetrate the meat and break down the enzymes.

2. When it's cooking time, preheat your oven to 400 degrees.

3. Brown each side of the loin in a cast-iron skillet until beautifully browned, about 5 minutes per side.

4. Then take that skillet and toss it in the oven for about 25 minutes. Remove from the oven and let sit for at least 15 minutes, but I wouldn't be mad at 20ish. The meat will continue to cook to that perfect pink doneness. A thermometer inserted into the meat should read about 145 degrees.

5. Slice into medallions. Serve with horseradish and or brown gravy.

**SEMI PRO TIP**: If you have time, marinate the beef the night before. All of the herbs and garlic fully penetrate the meat. At a minimum, at least an hour in advance! Again, I love doing as much as I can before any guests arrive so that I seem calm and relaxed in the kitchen. Panic mode can hit quickly when you're trying to get everything on the table at the same time. Keeping everyone's glasses full helps to distract from any panic you might be feeling. Yes, yes, drink up, everyone!

# HOT HONEY PIZZA

*Serves 4–6*

A nice pie slathered in a spicy honey drizzle! Need I say more? This recipe has every part of your palate covered: salt, fat, acid, heat, and sweet! (As a cookbook enthusiast, if you don't already own *Salt, Fat, Acid, Heat: Mastering the Elements of Good Cooking* by Samin Nosrat, do yourself a favor and ADD TO CART! It's both beautiful and insightful!)

| | |
|---|---|
| 2 cups flour (divided) | 1 cup pizza sauce |
| 1½ tsp. sugar | 2 cups shredded mozzarella |
| 1 pkg. instant yeast | ½ cup pepperoni |
| ½ tsp. salt | 4 slices bacon, crumbled |
| ½ tsp. garlic powder | HOT HONEY: |
| ¼ tsp. onion powder | ¼ cup honey |
| ¾ cup warm water | ¼ tsp. cayenne |
| 2 tbsp. olive oil, plus extra | a few dashes hot sauce |
| | ¼ tsp. salt |

1. In a large bowl, whisk together your dry ingredients: 1 cup flour, sugar, yeast, salt, garlic, and onion powder. Using a large spoon, add the water and olive oil and slowly mix together.

2. Your dough will be very wet at this point, so slowly add the other cup of flour. I usually work in about ¼ cup at a time. You want the dough to be sturdy and not too sticky. It should easily pull away from the bowl. At this point, remove from the bowl and continue to knead it on a floured surface until desired consistency.

3. Roll your dough into a uniform ball and add to a well-oiled bowl. Roll the dough ball in the oil to fully coat, and then cover the bowl and let rise to about double in size. About an hour.

4. Make the hot honey! Mix all of the ingredients together. Adjust the level of spice depending on how nuts you wanna go.

5. When the dough is close to ready, preheat your oven to 500 degrees.

6. You want your oven as hot as possible in order to get the pizza crispy. Place the baking sheet you plan on using in the oven to preheat the sheet as well. This helps with that crispy crust goodness! (We don't play with no floppy pizza.)

7. Roll out your dough to desired thickness. I like it pretty thin, about ¼ inch. Then, using a fork, poke holes all over the surface of the dough.

8. Add an even layer of the pizza sauce, shredded mozzarella, pepperoni, and bacon crumbles.

9. Bake for 12–15 minutes until all the cheese is bubbly and brown.

10. Slather on some hot honey! The more the better!

**SEMI PRO TIP**: Poking holes into the surface of the dough helps to ensure it won't bubble up and lose its shape while baking.

# Cocktails

If there's ONE thing I've learned about keeping a gathering of friends and family happy, it's keep the booze flowing. A libation to warm everyone up, keep things loosey-goosey, avoid any social awkwardness, and most importantly, keep yourself sane.

**"YOU CAN LEARN A LOT ABOUT A WOMAN BY GETTING SMASHED WITH HER."**
**—TOM WAITS**

# ROSE SANGRIA

*Serves 4*

Ah yes, the drink choice of the basic b**** during happy hour. Few things are better than hitting a patio with your pals, ordering several jugs of sangria, and getting smashed while basking in the blazing summer sun. I'll tell you what's in the direction of better…making your own! At home! That way you can be sure you're getting ALL the vitamins from the specially curated frozen fruit packages, it won't be overly diluted with juices, and also it will be spiked with a little something-something.

- 2 cups frozen peaches
- 2 cups frozen strawberries
- 1 bottle of rosé
- ½ cup triple sec
- 1½ cups sparkling water

Combine all ingredients in a large jug and keep cool until ready to serve. Serve over ice!

**SEMI PRO TIP**: I always opt for frozen fruit in my homemade sangrias. Less chopping, and the fruit can be a stand-in for the ice!

# THE COWBOY COCKTAIL

*Single serving*

For the rootin' tootin' cowboy in your life. He likes his drinks stiff with absolutely no fuss. Zero frills with this one. Careful…they'll knock you silly.

2(ish) shots of Jack Daniel's—
we like to eyeball it around our kitchen!

a mere splash of Diet Coke

ice

Serve this stiffy over ice, in a short glass. Again, nothing fancy. Don't even think about anything fancy while you're sipping on this.

**SEMI PRO TIP**: *Jack Daniel's is the whiskey of choice in my house, but experiment if you're feeling wild!*

# BLOODY CAESAR

*Single serving*

Oh, the joys of a Caesar, hands down one of my favorite cocktails of all time. This is the Canadian version of a Bloody Mary. I feel like any Canadian reading this is rolling their eyes that I'm actually putting this in a cookbook, because it's the most standard drink you get introduced to when you start your journey into legal consumption of booze. But I've found that it's really never made its way south of the Canadian border. I think what freaks people out is the Clamato juice. People lose their minds when you say there's clam juice in their vodka. Honestly, you don't even taste it. It's not remotely fishy, and it makes this drink much thinner than a typical Bloody Mary. Typically, it's always made with Clamato, but if that's not readily available where you live, fear not, you can make your own!

| | |
|---|---|
| 2 oz. vodka | celery salt for the rim |
| Homemade Clamato | lime |
| ice | celery stick |

## HOMEMADE CLAMATO

| | |
|---|---|
| 1 cup tomato juice | pinch of salt |
| ¼ cup clam juice | ¼ tsp. pepper |
| ½ tbsp. Worcestershire sauce | 1 oz. dill pickle juice |
| ½ tsp. tabasco | ¼ tsp. steak seasoning |
| 1 tsp. lemon juice (fresh) | |

Rim a large glass with the lime and celery salt. Fill the glass with ice, vodka, and the remaining ingredients. Give a good stir and adjust taste with more tabasco, salt, or pepper. Serve with a celery stalk!

**SEMI PRO TIP**: You can get very creative with the garnish of this drink. Typically, it's served with celery, but you could do crispy bacon, some fresh-cooked shrimp, grilled cheese, hot dog, whatever your little heart desires. This entire cocktail can be turned into brunch real quick!

# YE OLDE BOURBON CIDER

*Single serving*

I love a hot cocktail. Something about sitting outside in the cold and sipping on a warm boozy drink just makes me feel like I've finally been cast as the lead (or quirky neighbor) in a Hallmark Christmas movie. Yes, Hallmark, I am available and willing to drop my day rate. It's all very après-ski chic. This book is supposed to make you feel cozy and happy. Let's warm up over some piping hot bourbon!

| | |
|---|---|
| 1 oz. bourbon or whiskey—I used Bulleit bourbon | 1 tbsp. sugar |
| | 1 tsp. cinnamon |
| ¾ cup apple cider | I'm a big fan of using the mule mug for multiple drinks. I don't think it's limited to the Moscow mule. I'd use one here. |
| 1 tsp. honey | |
| cinnamon stick | |
| star anise | |

1. First, rim your glass with a healthy helping of the cinnamon/sugar rim. Just combine the cinnamon and sugar in a shallow dish. Run a slice of lime, or an apple, along the rim to get it wet so the cinnamon/sugar will adhere to the glass.

2. Bring the apple cider, honey, cinnamon stick, and star anise to a simmer. Allow to simmer about 5–10 minutes.

3. Drop a shot of your favorite bourbon in the glass and top with your delicious warm spiced apple cider.

# PINEAPPLE MOJITO

*Single serving*

Fresh 'n' fruity, baby! Fresh herbs in your cocktail glass feels oh so chic. At least to me, who is normally drinking wine from a box in the fridge. I love the added sweetness and acidity from the pineapple. Drink 45 of these and then tweet me!

½ cup pineapple juice

5 fresh mint leaves

1 tsp. sugar

1 tbsp. lime juice

1 oz. white rum

Muddle together the mint, sugar, and lime juice. Pour into a highball glass filled with ice, drop in your shot of rum, top with pineapple juice, give it a swirl and then down the hatch, amigo!

# BLACKBERRY SAGE SMASH

*Single serving*

I feel like a tried, tested, and true mixologist when I make this cocktail. Muddling together the plump juicy berries with some freshly torn sage smells amazing! So fresh and light and also Instagram-worthy.

8 blackberries

5 sage leaves, torn

2 tsp. sugar

2 oz. gin

1 oz. lime juice

1 cup soda water

ice

dried sage leaf (optional, but good for the 'Gram)

1. Combine the blackberries, sage, sugar, and lime juice. Smash into a paste with the back of a spoon or mortar and pestle. Breaking up the sage will release all of the delicious oils and mix with the juices of the blackberries and the lime.

2. Fill a highball glass with ice. Pour the gin over the ice. Add the blackberry/sage mixture and top with soda water.

**SEMI PRO TIP:** If you have dried sage leaves on hand, using one as a garnish looks so cool. You can light it on fire and blow it out, so you have a fancy smoking drink when serving to your guests.

Dried sage is also good for ridding your home of bad energy. Voodoo witchcraft! I swear by it. Just open all the windows so the bad energy can escape!

# COCO-LIME MARGS

*Serves 4–6*

I've literally never met a margarita I didn't like. I welcome them all into my house and my temple, a.k.a. my body. The velvetiness from the cream of coconut makes this drink taste as if a piña colada and a margarita fell in love at an all-inclusive resort in Cancun and had a sassy drunk baby.

Makes about 4-6 glasses, depending on what kinda mood you're in. I don't make blended-ice drinks by the single glass. If I'm making these, everyone's drinking 'em!

1 can cream of coconut (I used Coco Lopez)

1 cup tequila

½ cup Key West lime juice

¼ cup triple sec

1 tbsp. lime zest

lime for garnish

2 cups ice

1. In a blender, combine the cream of coconut, tequila, Key West lime juice, lime zest, triple sec, and ice. Blend until the ice has turned into slush.

2. Pour into a margarita glass and garnish with a lime wedge!

# The Jams

I've always felt that, more than anything, your outfit and the music set the mood. Since this isn't a fashion magazine, I can only guide you on the tunes. With the help of some of my favorite people, I've created some badass playlists. I sent out a bunch of texts and emails so I could have a solid variety from people whose ears and vibes I trust! I broke these playlists into some categories that I figured could suit multiple scenarios. Happy hosting!

BRUNCH

DRINKS

DATE NIGHT

GIRLS NIGHT

BBQ

DINNER PARTY

# Final Touches

Just a few things to keep in mind while you're the hostest with the mostest.

Keep the drinks flowing. Even better, set up a bar cart so people can help themselves and take a little stress off yourself. I always designate my husband as bartender, but he always forgets after he's given out the first round. So, having all the booze accessible is key. Plus, I've always found it makes everyone feel way more comfortable and relaxed in your house. People like having something to do!

Prepare whatever you can in advance and clean as you go! That way the house doesn't look like a bomb went off and you don't look even the slightest bit frazzled while people start to gather around the kitchen as you cook. It always goes that way. Everyone loves to kick it in the kitchen. Put out some easy light snacks to keep everyone at bay.

If there's a dish you're going to be serving and it can be made a day or two ahead of time and popped in the oven or re-heated, go for it! Then it won't feel like you're juggling a million things on the day of the party. Peel and dice your veggies so they're ready to go when you start cooking.

I keep a giant bowl on the countertop when I'm cooking and use it as my garbage bowl. Veggie shavings, seeds and pits from fruits and veggies, and discarded bits of food and trash can just hang there before getting tossed out at the end. I saw Rachael Ray do this years ago, and I've adopted it myself. It's much easier than walking back and forth to the trash can.

Have paper towels and ice on hand. You don't wanna run out of these babies. There's always a mess to clean and a cup that needs refreshing.

Fresh flowers are such a cheap and pretty way to add a personal touch. I always used to think having flowers was SO fancy or that I needed to only have them on certain occasions or gifted to me. HELL NAHHHH, buy your damn self some flowers and display them around the house. Trader Joe's is my favorite florist.

Let people help you. People love feeling useful. Don't feel the need to be the hero. Delegate some duties and have someone chop veggies for you or help to set the table or wash some dishes. It took me a few dinner parties to learn this one. I never wanted anyone to feel like they needed to lift a finger, when

in fact it's the opposite. And if people offer to bring something, let them know what you want, whether it's dessert or booze.

Finally, just be ready to go with the flow and don't put so much pressure on yourself. You've got this!

# Acknowledgments

While writing a cookbook can be a monumental project, writing the acknowledgements is perhaps more stressful in the event that I'm a dumbass and forget someone. If I do, just know that I love you and appreciate you more than the people I've listed. It's like our little inside wink, wink. Seriously, I really hope I haven't forgotten anyone!

First and foremost, a gigantic thank you to Jacob Hoye at Permuted Press and Amanda Luedeke at MacGregor Literary. You guys both took a chance on a girl that comes from the world of wrestling and just desperately wanted to make a cookbook. Not exactly easy to connect the dots on that one, but you guys both believed in my vision and my passion. And, most importantly to me, you just let me be me in my writing and all of the creative aspects that went into this book. I owe you both a huge dinner party!! My agent David Koonin at CAA, thank you for always helping me to find the perfect opportunities to create and always supporting whatever ideas I happen to manically call you about. There will be plenty more. Get ready!!

Gaby Duong, the incredibly talented photographer that captured all of my food to make it look like an actual chef might have actually participated in making these meals. You're a sweet gem of a woman! And Jackie Sobon, my amazing food stylist that also realllllllyyyyy stepped it up to makes these meals look profesh as all hell. Also, you are an insanely talented cookbook author yourself and I highly suggest anyone here looking for some great vegan meals to check her stuff out! The fact you still aided me in making my non-vegan meals meant the world to me, because, man oh man, did you ever makes these photoshoots go a hell of a lot more smoothly. Imagine if you weren't there? We'd still be shooting, I'm positive. We did the photos for this book over the course of 4 days, and that included all of the photos of me pretending to be cute while cooking. It was so daunting and scary to just put our heads down and cook and photograph and try to schedule each meal appropriately, but without Gaby, Jackie, and, of course, Savannah Brady. Sweet, sweet Savannah, you were the extra eyes, ears and hands that I needed for this shoot. Also, a morale boost and a hell of a playlist aficionado. Leslie Homan, you stepped in to not only help with my makeup (THANKYO-UUUUUUU!!) but also stayed around to assist in

anything we needed. You and Savannah really know your way around a charcuterie board, and now its forever immortalized within the pages of this book. Speaking of makeup Brian Valentine, thank you for "beating my face to the gawds" as the kids on the ol Instagram would say. I knew right away you were the man for the job once I realized this mug was going to be photographed. THANK YOU! Clayton Ferrell and Cailey McCalister, thank you for your edits on this book. You both gave me such peace of mind that two true pros actually sifted through this and made sense of anything dumb I wrote. Huge sigh of relief. For all of my cool ass friends that helped me curate the playlists in this book, you are so appreciated!! I went to some of my most trusted sources to get a great variety of smooth jams from people with good ears! So, thanks to Jon Good, Erik Paquette, Tex Paquette, Marilyn Ryan, Sean Marshall, Matt Farmer, Savannah Brady (again!), Nicky Sampogna, Brie and Nikki Bella, Saraya Bevis, Nia Jax, Michael Cole, and Jacob Ullman. You all rule very hard.

Thanks to my mom and dad for always supporting all of my ventures. Mom, thanks for the dinners out, the meals made, and recipes passed down. Wish you could have been here to help me cook all of these up. But you finding all of Nanny's hand written recipes gave me so much inspiration while I was making this book!

To my husband, Jon. Thank you for fully and truly supporting me in whatever I want to do. You often believe in me more than I do myself and it makes me feel like I can really make anything happen. And now there's a real book!! What?!? You're always a willing participant when I need the meal to be taste tested, or make a run to the grocery store. You were an angel on freaking earth during the photoshoot because I would give you a list of very random ingredients and you always returned with them all. You know how to navigate the grocery aisles like a pro. I'll make you well-done steaks with a side of ketchup for life. Anyone with a problem with that, take it up with him. The man likes what he likes!

And to the sweet little baby currently growing inside me with your own amazing little heartbeat!! I can't wait to cook for you and have staple meals you beg me to cook for you! I'm so excited for all of the amazing traditions we'll be able to have together. I love you so much already. And wow, am I ever glad I finished writing this book before I got pregnant. Because otherwise it would just be a two chapter book about toast with peanut butter and bananas, and things to top a saltine cracker with.

Thank you so so much to everyone that helped me out with this book. It really means the world to me.

Renée
xo

185

# About the Author

Renée Paquette has been working in television for over a decade. She was the first female commentator for *Monday Night Raw* on USA network, and a trailblazer in her own right in the world of sports entertainment and broadcasting. She has been featured on *Total Divas* on E! and Fox Sports, continually expanding her resume.

A proud Canadian, Renée grew up in a family of food lovers, and she loves nothing more than stepping out on a culinary limb in hopes that her food creations will be the talk of the table. As a first-time author, she's really hoping this book paves the way for many more!